DEMOCRAZY

SA'S TWENTY-YEAR TRIP

TEXT BY MIKE WILLS

JACANA

1994   PAGE 08

1996   PAGE 18

1998   PAGE 30

2000   PAGE 64

2002   PAGE 84

2004   PAGE 97

THE MANDELA YEARS   THE MBEKI YEARS

PAGE 15 | 1995

PAGE 25 | 1997

PAGE 58 | 1999

PAGE 73 | 2001

PAGE 91 | 2003

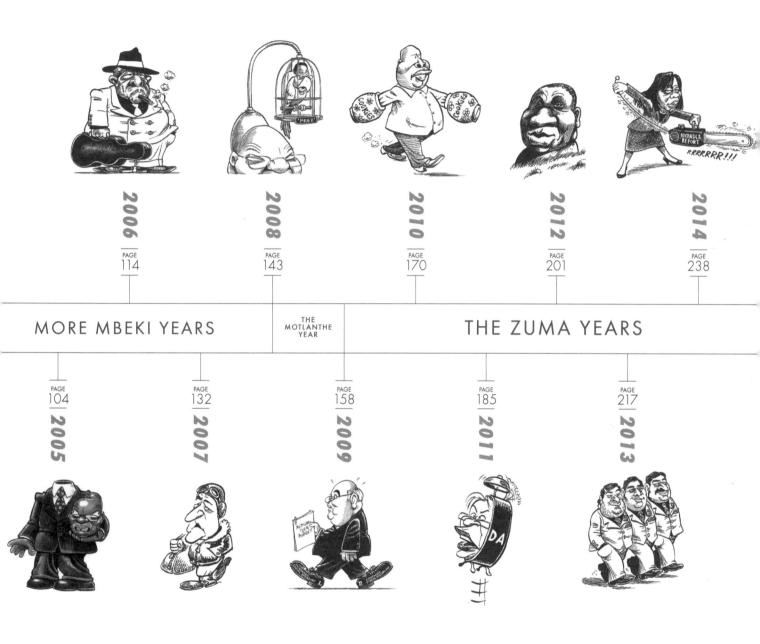

2006

2008

2010

2012

2014

MORE MBEKI YEARS

THE
MOTLANTHE
YEAR

THE ZUMA YEARS

2005

2007

2009

2011

2013

PREFACE

1994 was the birth of our democracy. It was history in the making, history in the cartooning, as we stumbled and staggered our way into this New South Africa. The whole enterprise felt permanently perilous – always on the brink of falling apart and yet, against the odds, just about holding together.

Our society still feels like that sometimes – fragmented and united in equal measure and constantly both momentous and on the fringe of craziness – which is a space just made for a cartoonist!

In these 20 years of South African democracy I have done more than 4 000 cartoons for the *Mail & Guardian*, *Sowetan*, *Sunday Times*, *The Times* and Independent Newspapers. This collection has only 450 of them but, viewed together, I believe them to be a different kind of record of the road we have travelled since 1994.

There has never been a shortage of material for me to draw; in fact there have been many days when South Africa was crazier than anything my imagination could conjure up and often the hardest challenge has been to find that element of humour essential for effective cartooning in such debilitating events.

The place of the cartoonist in our politics has changed markedly over the 20 years. It felt like a privilege to capture Nelson Mandela, warts and all. He was an epic man with a palpable sense of tolerance and good humour.

Thabo Mbeki was made of sterner stuff – quite literally. He rarely smiled and was prickly with criticism but, to his credit, never threatened me, or any other cartoonist who was publicly skewering his personality or his policies.

In the Zuma era that has changed and, more times than I am comfortable with, my cartoons have moved from being a commentary on the story to becoming the story, as the president fired off, to date unfulfilled, substantial lawsuits.

I am grateful to all the editors who have continued to publish my cartoons in the face of such heavy-handed aggression. They have defended the essential place of freedom of expression in our constitution.

I am also very grateful to my good friend, the wonderful Kenyan cartoonist Gado (www.gadocartoons.com) for readily agreeing to my using the same title for this book that he had already used in an East African publication. There simply is no better word to sum up the extraordinary ride we have been on for the past two decades than democrazy.

ZAPIRO

Freedom Day, 27 April 2014

1994 THE ELECTION

In April 1994, under the glare of an unprecedented gathering of global media, the man running the historic first democratic elections, judge Johann Kriegler, loomed hawk-like out of our television sets proclaiming, "We're ready, you're ready, let's do it." He was half right, we were ready but the IEC certainly wasn't.

The IEC probably never stood a chance, given they were flying blind with no voters' roll and the IFP only joining the ballot eight days before polling.

The voting ran for four days instead of the planned three. The counting stuttered along for ten more agonising days until a negotiated plan was passed off as free and fair just in time for the global glitterati to descend on the Union Buildings to proclaim and acclaim President Nelson Mandela.

1994–1999 THE MANDELA YEARS

Nelson Mandela's inauguration on 10 May 1994 represented a spectacular new dawn on a huge pile of old problems.

Mandela's predecessor FW de Klerk joined him in the government of national unity (GNU) as one of two deputy presidents; Thabo Mbeki was the other.

The harsh realities of delivering widespread economic change soon became starkly apparent to housing minister Joe Slovo and Jay Naidoo who was responsible for the much-touted Reconstruction and Development Programme, or RDP.

Finance minister Derek Keys, former head of Gencor, suddenly resigned in July 1994 – Mandela rushed another senior businessman, Chris Liebenberg of Nedcor, into this place.

There was considerable resistance to the new dispensation, especially in former Model-C classrooms. A Supreme Court ruling was required to force Potgietersrus Primary School in Limpopo to allow black pupils to enrol. The first sixteen black children were subjected to abuse. and were protected by police officers.

In the early days the government seemed beset by crises that only Mandela's intervention could resolve.

Among the many problems Mandela inherited, the crime rate seemed to be the most intimidating,

The appalling number of rapes and the seemingly complete inability of the justice system, or of broader South African society, to effectively tackle the problem were giving the nation a shameful reputation as one of the world's worst for gender violence.

The few crooks who were caught seemed to end up back on the streets alarmingly quickly.

The controversial Winnie Mandela was appointed deputy minister of arts, culture, science and technology. She immediately clashed with her minister, the IFP's Ben Ngubane, and could never shake the stories surrounding her involvement in the death of 14-year-old activist Stompie Seipei in 1989.

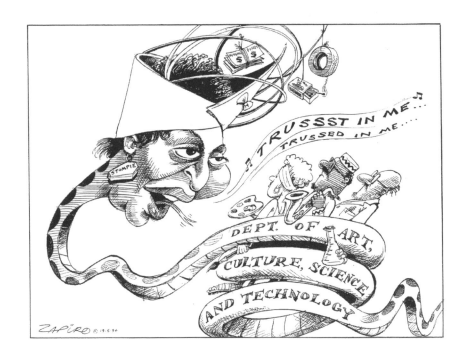

The GNU was a CODESA creation designed to last until the constitution was finalised. Both the Nats and the IFP took cabinet posts under the arrangement, but they blew hot and cold on whether they should be riding this wildebeest.

The 1995 rugby world cup triumph of Francois Pienaar's (and Nelson Mandela's) Springboks proved to be a high point of post-election euphoria and reconciliation.

In August 1995, Mandela visited 94-year-old Betsie Verwoerd, the widow of apartheid's architect Hendrik Verwoerd, in the Northern Cape whites-only enclave of Orania. It was the most famous, and controversial, of his trademark gestures of reconciliation.

Mandela also travelled to take tea with his former jailer President PW Botha in the Wilderness where Botha lived – both literally and figuratively. Botha was characeristically combative and warned Mandela "to not awaken the tiger of black and white nationalism".

The Truth and Reconciliation Commission (TRC) was established in 1995. Justice minister Dullah Omar was in no mood to provide a free pass for former cabinet ministers like Magnus Malan and Adriaan Vlok, and SAP commissioner Johann van der Merwe.

Mandela understood the symbolic power of sport especially in a golden age which included Bafana Bafana's triumph in the 1996 African Cup of Nations on home soil. He happily wore national kit of any kind – even if the sports, like cricket or rugby, which was run by the highly controversial former fertiliser king Louis Luyt, were perceived to belong to the apartheid era.

Mandela moved too slowly for some in taking action against struggle luminaries who faced allegations of impropriety. Rev. Allan Boesak was scheduled to become South Africa's ambassador to the UN in Geneva in 1994 when he was accused of corruption and fraud in connection with donations from Scandinavia. The affair dragged on without decisive intervention until the appointment was finally withdrawn. Health minister Dr Nkosazana Dlamini-Zuma commissioned *Sarafina II*, a R14-million musical produced by Mbongeni Ngema, that was savaged for its mixed messages on HIV and its hugely inflated budget.

Inkatha leader Mangosuthu Buthelezi was both inside the government as minister of home affairs and outside it with constant demands for special constitutional treatment for the Zulu nation, especially on the thorny issue of the right to carry traditional weapons.

Inkatha was just one of many problems for Cyril Ramaphosa, who, as chair of the Constitutional Assembly, was driving the drafting process for the founding document of the new democracy but, by May 1996, the new constitution was agreed upon and Ramaphosa had stolen a march on Thabo Mbeki, his rival for the succession to Mandela.

The tenuous GNU finally fell apart in May 1996 when FW de Klerk led the Nats out of the cabinet with the ink barely dry on the new constitution.

Mandela's reception on his international travels was more akin to a rock star than a head of state.

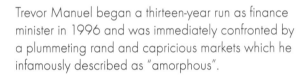
Trevor Manuel began a thirteen-year run as finance minister in 1996 and was immediately confronted by a plummeting rand and capricious markets which he infamously described as "amorphous".

Manuel also faced serious divisions within the alliance about the conservative nature of his policies.

Significant political organisations from the past – like Clarence Makwetu's PAC and Mosibudi Mangena's AZAPO – failed to adapt to post-liberation realities.

In June 1997, Roelf Meyer broke away from the Nats and formed the United Democratic Movement with Bantu Holomisa, who fled the ANC.

More than ever the nation's fortunes seemed to rest entirely on the shoulders of Nelson Mandela.

PUBLIC PERCEPTION MAP
PRICE: $1·00 (=R947·50)
WITCHCRAFT ZONE
CONSULTANT HEAVEN
HIJACKIA
SOL'S BRIBERY CENTRE
HEADLESS CHICKEN STATE
INDEPENDENT KINGDOM OF MANGO
WHERE'S THAT AGAIN ?
CHAOTICA
PAGADLAND
TOUR GUIDE
SA: OFFICIAL VERSION
SOWETAN 27·11·96 ZAPIRO©

M&G 24-12-96 © ZAPIRO

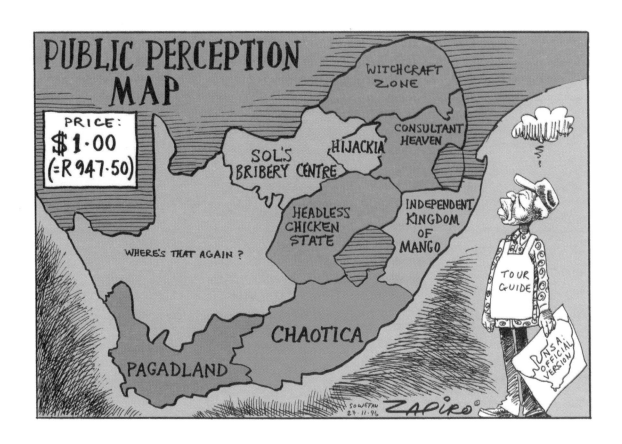

After several policy and personnel changes, police commissioner George Fivaz and safety and security minister Sydney Mufamadi were still unable to get to grips with crime.

Justice minister Dullah Omar and Sipho Mzimela at correctional services weren't doing much better.

Prisons commissioner Khulekani Sithole sparked widespread condemnation with his harebrained scheme to house prisoners in mine shafts. Sithole was later axed after a parliamentary committee inquiry revealed cronyism and a private soccer team being run with departmental funds.

Trevor Manuel's 1997 budget was all things to all men but one year later, amidst a global emerging markets crisis, things weren't looking quite so miraculous.

The RDP was out and Thabo Mbeki's brainchild GEAR (the Growth Employment and Redistribution programme) was in.

At the labour ministry Tito Mboweni was also struggling to master a ring full of sound and fury while some big SA businesses – Anglo American, Old Mutual and SAB among them – were scrambling off to London for their primary stock listings.

South Africa's foreign policy seemed to be permanently tenuous and conflicted. Foreign minister Alfred Nzo was known only for his ability to do and say nothing, Kader Asmal was wrestling with the dubious morality of arms trading, Thabo Mbeki was pursuing the chimera of the African Renaissance and deputy minister Aziz Pahad was constantly compromised by tough issues such as East Timor.

As early as 1995 the seeds were being sown by defence minister Joe Modise and his deputy Ronnie Kasrils for the massive equipment upgrade for the SANDF, which would lead into the tawdry web of the still unresolved Arms Deal scandal.

Not even Mandela's legendary charms could win
Cape Town the right to host the 2004 Olympics.
Athens got the nod to the sound of shattered dreams
on the Grand Parade.

In March 1998 Bill Clinton made the first-ever US presidential visit to South Africa in the midst of a deepening domestic scandal around his sexual involvement with White House intern Monica Lewinsky.

Mandela was out of the country when the SANDF launched itself into Lesotho on 22 September 1998, for reasons best known to acting president Buthelezi. The South African forces got a bloody nose in the ill-planned invasion in support of prime minister Pakalitha Mosisili's government.

The escalating conflict in the DRC was only the biggest of many conflicts that undermined Thabo Mbeki's grandiose visions for the continent's future.

Another complicating factor in international relations was the arrest of foreign affairs official and former MK operative, Robert McBride, in Mozambique on mysterious and murky charges of gun-running. The strange affair failed to compromise McBride's career and he would continue to find different ways to be a complicating factor throughout the 20 years of democracy.

THE RESURRECTION OF ROBERT McBRIDE

Winnie Madikizela-Mandela had been dismissed as a cabinet minister in 1995 after allegations of corruption, she and Nelson divorced in 1996, she constantly flouted party discipline and she was being subpoenaed to appear in front of the TRC, yet Winnie retained her position as head of the ANC Women's League and remained a prominent presence.

The TRC, chaired by Archbishop Desmond Tutu, was a constant theme of the Mandela years. Its first hearings, in April 1996, were opened with a prayer from Tutu.

FW de Klerk appeared twice before the commission – apologising "once and for all" for apartheid and the hurt caused by its policies but denying National Party responsibility for murder, torture and other gross human rights abuses.

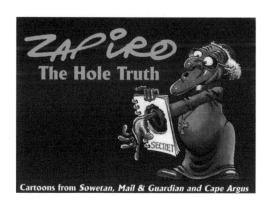

The detailed evidence
of Vlakplaas commander
Eugene de Kock, who
became known as Prime
Evil, posed serious
questions for National
Party leaders and
apartheid-era securocrats.

Former State President PW Botha defied a subpoena to appear before the commission, calling it a "circus" and claiming poor health even though he had publicly started a new relationship with a woman 25 years his junior.

The sole Nat cabinet member to confess human rights abuses and to be granted amnesty by the TRC was former law and order minister Adriaan Vlok.

No TRC hearing gathered as much attention as the appearance of Winnie Madikizela-Mandela. She faced a range of serious accusations concerning the activities of the Mandela United football club, who acted as her bodyguards, and her connections to the murders of Soweto doctor Abu Baker Asvat and 14-year-old activist Stompie Seipei.

In October 1997, 'People's Poet' Mzwakhe Mbuli, a prominent anti-apartheid voice who had performed at Mandela's inauguration, was caught robbing a bank with two of his former bodyguards. He claimed he was framed but was sentenced to ten years in prison.

The education system under minister Sibusiso Bengu was an area of serious under-performance and alarming corruption.

Opposition politics were changing. De Klerk resigned as leader of the (now) New National Party in 1997 to be replaced by Marthinus van Schalkwyk, and Tony Leon was trying to darken the Democratic Party.

May 1998 marked an anniversary of sorts for the Nats and Marthinus van Schalkwyk whose youthful appearance and lack of experience had earned him the disdainful nickname of Kortbroek.

PAC leader and
Methodist bishop
Stanley Mogoba
endorsed amputation of
limbs as a punishment
for certain crimes.

Inevitably the
opposition was
overshadowed by
Mandela's personality
and agenda.

The TRC's report was finally delivered to President Mandela on 29 October 1998. Its findings on the actions of the ANC provoked outrage from some in the party, including secretary-general Kgalema Motlanthe.

Reconciliation took a back seat with the killing during Easter 1998 of six-month-old Angelina Zwane by a ricochet rifle shot from a farmer's son while she was being carried across his smallholding near Benoni. An estimated 10 000 attended her funeral.

In March 1999, former UDF leader Rev. Allan Boesak was found guilty of fraud in connection with Scandinavian donor funding and sent to jail. During the case, he declined to give evidence in his own defence.

Madiba's 80th birthday on 18 June 1998 was marked by widespread celebration.

Mandela's 80th also marked his marriage to Graça Machel, an event he had desperately tried and failed to keep secret.

Mandela resisted all entreaties to stay on for a second presidential term. Thabo Mbeki was the clear favourite to succeed him, but he was not without rivals. Mandela reportedly favoured Cyril Ramaphosa and was rumoured to be deliberately handing Mbeki the most awkward issues to resolve as a way of tainting his record as a Mr Fix-It.

The increasingly dictatorial tendencies of Zimbabwean president Robert Mugabe were attracting heightened criticism inside South Africa. In 1999 he cracked down hard on media freedom.

Mandela's final State of the Nation Address was a moment of great emotion but not without its dark shadows.

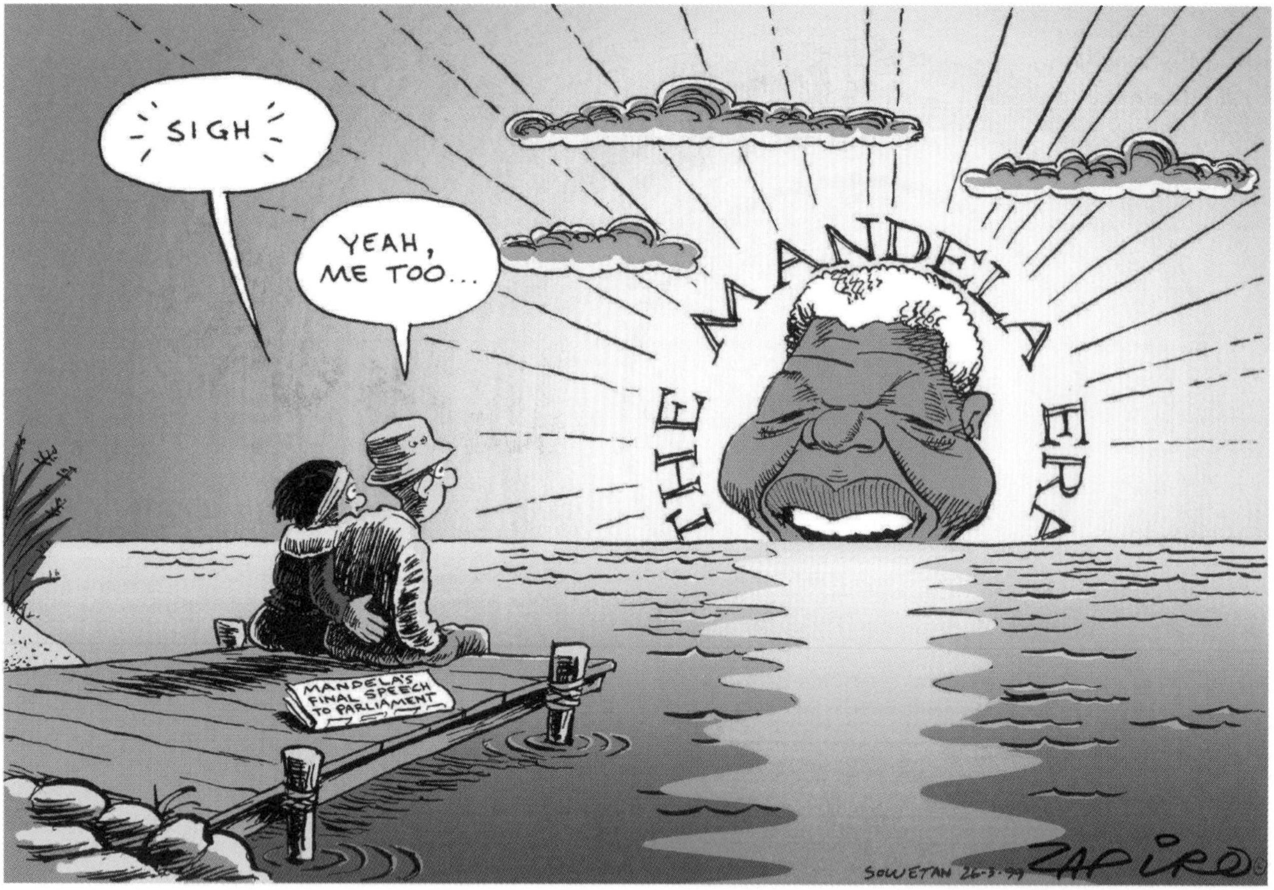
SIGH
YEAH, ME TOO...
THE MANDELA ERA
MANDELA'S FINAL SPEECH TO PARLIAMENT
SOWETAN 26-3-99 ZAPIRO

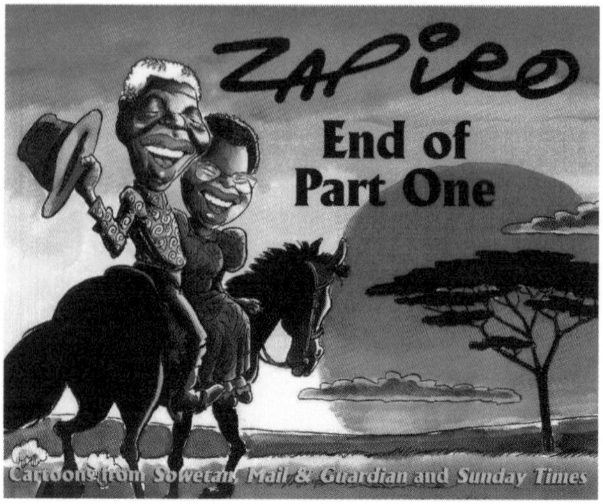
ZAPIRO
End of Part One
Cartoons from Sowetan, Mail & Guardian and Sunday Times

The second democratic election in 1999 inevitably lacked the drama and intensity of the first one.

The results saw Thabo Mbeki taking power with 66% of the vote – the DA grew to 9% and the Nats' support was cut by half.

President Mbeki began his first term with a reputation as a no-nonsense, pragmatic man of action.

Cartoons from *Sowetan, Mail & Guardian* and *Sunday Times*

Mbeki's vow to root out corruption was set back when one of his appointees, Mpumalanga premier Ndaweni Mahlangu, infamously remarked that "it is acceptable for politicians to lie". He was defending his decision to reappoint three disgraced MECs who had lied in connection with allegations of fraud and corruption.

Within his first year, Mbeki and party chairperson Mosiuoa Lekota were already sidelining the unions and the communist party.

59

New education minister Kader Asmal inherited a mass of ineffective policies to which he promptly added the ambitious OBE (outcomes-based education) syllabus.

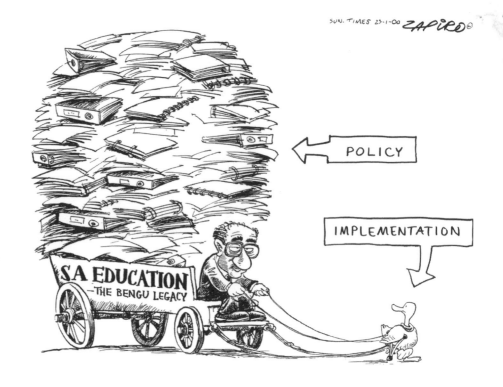

In spite of favourable global conditions, the local economy stubbornly failed to deliver widespread benefits.

AWB leader Eugène Terre'Blanche was sentenced to six years in prison for assault of a petrol-station worker and attempted murder of a security guard. He would serve three years of the term.

The Nats' colourful former foreign affairs minister Pik Botha publicly declared his support for President Mbeki and the ANC in 2000, although he later said that he never actually joined the party.

President Mbeki faced allegations that he was more interested in playing on the world stage than the domestic one.

For Mbeki, a litany of problems had left his image in tatters one year after taking office.

The economic and political crisis in Zimbabwe, and Robert Mugabe's increasingly desperate attempts to cling to power, tested the entire region. Mbeki's appointed observers found Zimbabwe's 2000 elections to be free and fair in the face of plenty of evidence to the contrary.

In April 2000, Indian police announced that that they had tapes of national cricket captain Hansie Cronjé arranging to fix matches.

Cartoons from *Sowetan, Mail & Guardian and Sunday Times*

After initial denials, Cronjé confessed and testified to the subsequent King Commission about the role of Satan in his downfall.

THE BAD NEWS IS YOUR SON CHEATS, TELLS LIES AND BULLIES HIS PEERS INTO DOING BAD THINGS.

PRINCIPAL

THE GOOD NEWS IS HE COULD BECOME SOUTH AFRICA'S CRICKET CAPTAIN.

July 2000 saw another sporting disaster when a wayward abstention vote from Kiwi Charlie Dempsey deprived SA of the hosting rights for the 2006 FIFA World Cup.

From the beginning of his presidency, Thabo Mbeki and his new health minister Manto Tshabalala-Msimang resisted conventional science on HIV/Aids and aligned themselves with controversial "denialists". The government at first refused, and then obstructed, the provision of antiretroviral drugs like AZT, which were especially effective in preventing mother-to-child HIV transmission. Both Mbeki and Tshabalala-Msimang believed that poverty and diet were the key issues to be tackled.

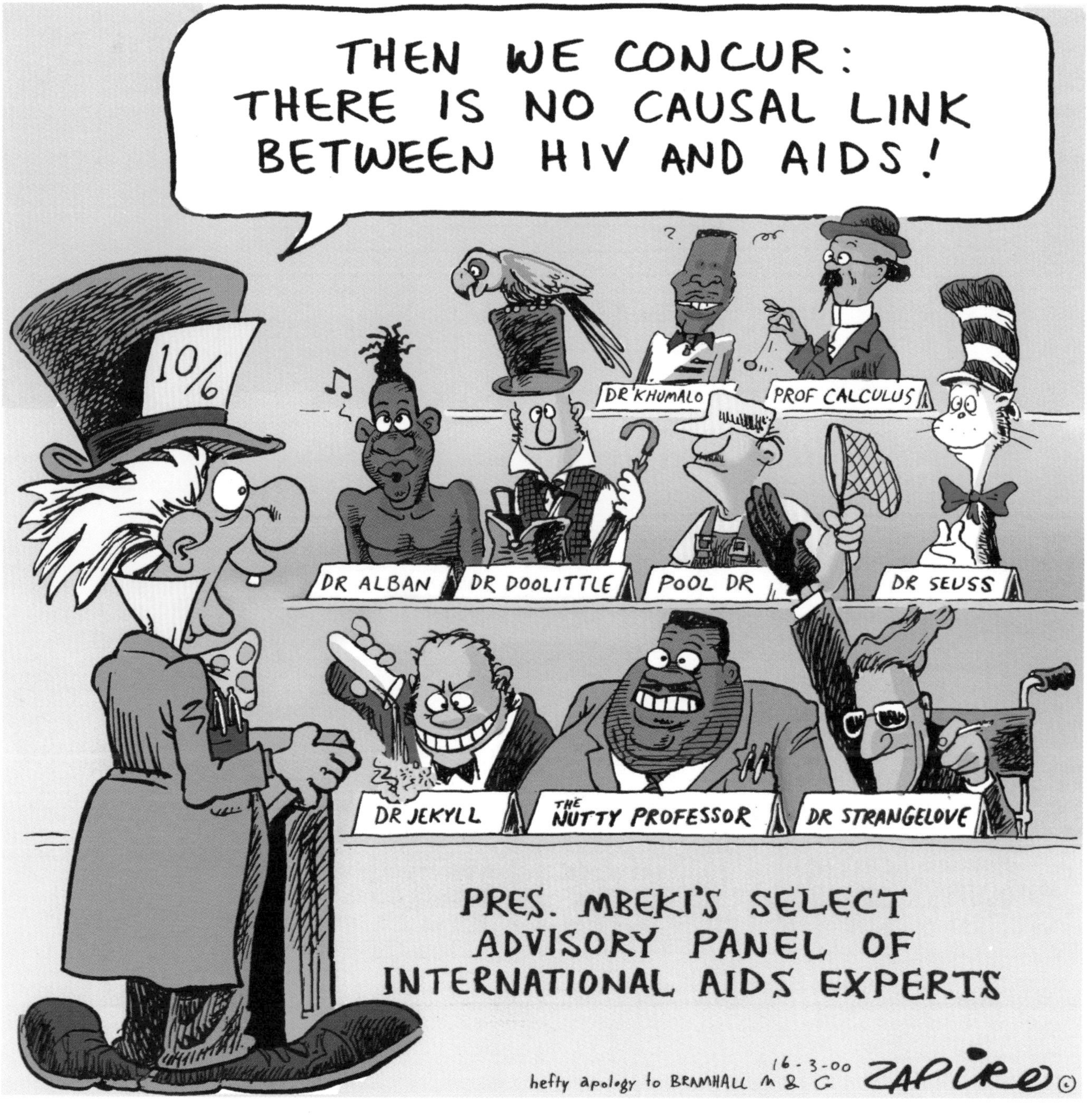
THEN WE CONCUR: THERE IS NO CAUSAL LINK BETWEEN HIV AND AIDS!
10/6
DR KHUMALO
PROF CALCULUS
DR ALBAN
DR DOOLITTLE
POOL DR
DR SEUSS
DR JEKYLL
THE NUTTY PROFESSOR
DR STRANGELOVE
PRES. MBEKI'S SELECT ADVISORY PANEL OF INTERNATIONAL AIDS EXPERTS
16-3-00
hefty apology to BRAMHALL M&G
ZAPIRO ©

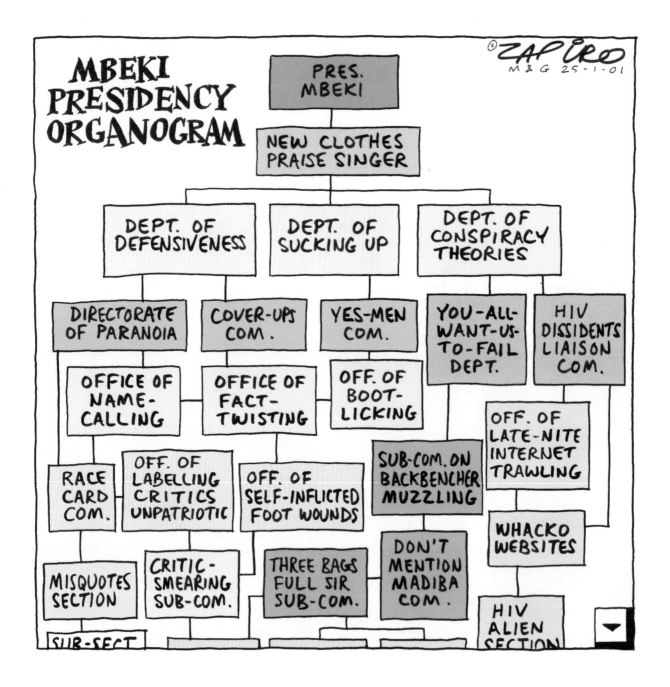

Mbeki had developed a reputation for defensives and surrounding himself with uncritical voices. Tony Leon recounts that Nelson Mandela drew his attention to this cartoon when they were discussing Mbeki's presidency during a meeting nearly a year after it was first published.

WHEW!
WHAT IS IT, DEAR?
I HAD A DREAM... IN MY DREAM I SPOKE TO THABO IN FRONT OF THE WHOLE NATION!
I TOLD HIM: "CRITICISM IS THE LIFE-BLOOD OF THE MOVEMENT! DON'T SURROUND YOURSELF WITH YES-MEN!"
BUT MADIBA, THAT'S WHAT YOU ACTUALLY TOLD HIM... AT THE ANC NATIONAL CONFERENCE IN MAFIKENG IN 1997.
OH, RIGHT. I DID.
MAYBE HE DREAMT HE DIDN'T HEAR ME...
GO TO SLEEP, DEAR.
ZAPIRO

Corruption was feeling institutionalised.

Another form of denialism also felt institutionalised.

WHITES WHO NEVER BENEFITTED FROM APARTHEID:

SOWETAN 5-9-00 ZAPIRO

STATE OF THE NATION: READY FOR AN UPGRADE

Mr Delivery

PUTT PUTT

MADE BY BOEING

WOOOSH

Mr Delivery

ZAPIRO © SOWETAN 7-2-01

Mbeki attempted to boost his image in the 2001 State of the Nation Address.

The blunt and coarse safety and security minister Steve Tshwete loomed large in the Mbeki administration. At one point he was even acting president.

Tshwete and his police commissioner Jackie Selebi were reluctant to release the full statistical details of the nation's crime problem.

Zimbabwe was sinking into economic collapse and political repression, but Mbeki and his foreign affairs minister Nkosazana Dlamini-Zuma always favoured cautious negotiation with the Mugabe government.

The government became increasingly critical of media coverage.

In May 2001, the air was thick with plots. Steve Tshwete publicly claimed that former politicians turned businessmen - Tokyo Sexwale, Mathews Phosa and Cyril Ramaphosa - were part of a conspiracy aimed at undermining the presidency and said they were being investigated by state intelligence agencies.

On the other side of the political fence, the DP, led by Tony Leon, and the NNP, led by Marthinus van Schalkwyk, had come together to form a tempestuous and short-lived partnership in the Democratic Alliance.

The NNP eventually walked out of the DA in 2001 and the ANC, represented by Mosioua Lekota, went into an unlikely alliance with the remnants of the party that had created apartheid.

Former Nat cabinet minister Piet Koornhof who, at one point, was directly responsible for the forced removals policy, also leapt across the political divide.

By 2001, the Arms Deal (which cost an estimated R38bn in 1999 values) had become a running sore of corruption allegations, denials, ineffectual probes, inappropriate equipment and misplaced priority. Even the initially promising Special Investigating Unit process under judge Willem Heath had been hamstrung.

Education minister Kader Asmal
launched the merger of universities
and technikons.

Brothers Chippy and Schabir Shaik featured heavily in the muddy swirl of Arms Deal accusations. Chippy was suspended from his position in the defence ministry, while Schabir was arrested and charged in connection with financial assistance given to ANC chairperson Jacob Zuma.

The first high profile ANC casualty from the Arms Deal was struggle luminary and party chief whip Tony Yengeni who was arrested in connection with the "assisted" purchase of a Mercedes SUV.

Yengeni published full-page advertisements in major newspapers (except the *Sunday Times*, which broke the story) proclaiming his innocence, but he would be convicted three years later.

The government seemed no closer to bringing the seemingly lawless and unsafe taxi industry under any form of sustainable regulation or control.

In spite of Trevor Manuel and public enterprises minister Jeff Radebe doing a business-friendly dance, the rand took a hammering in late 2001, falling 26% in less than three months, sparking President Mbeki to launch the Myburgh Commission of investigation.

As the ANC celebrated its 90th birthday and its eighth year in power, economic policy remained fiscally conservative in the face of persistent inequalities.

Mbeki ruthlessly overrode economic policy objections from COSATU's Zwelinzima Vavi and the SACP's Jeremy Cronin.

Winnie Madikizela-Mandela was rarely out of the headlines (and the cartoons).

In July 2002, Madikizela-Mandela went on trial for fraud and theft in connection with money taken from a funeral fund. In April 2003, she was found guilty and sentenced to prison. On appeal, the conviction for theft was overturned and she was given a suspended sentence for the fraud.

In 2002 South African politics was tainted by a spate of floor-crossing, a constitutionally permitted period in which elected members could change parties and keep their seats in parliament where Frene Ginwala was the speaker and presiding officer. These MPs became known as "crosstitutes" and the demeaning practice was finally abolished in 2009.

On 1 June 2002,
disgraced Protea skipper
Hansie Cronjé died in a
plane crash sparking an
outpouring of exoneration.

Cartoons from *Sowetan*, *Mail & Guardian* and *Sunday Times*

"Cause of death" had become a politicised line on any certificate and in any obituary. Former ANC Youth League leader and deputy cabinet minister Peter Mokaba succumbed to Aids-related pneumonia in 2002, but he had claimed that HIV and Aids were a "Western imperialist plot".

Mbeki's predecessor had admitted to his government's failings on HIV and, in retirement, was determined to rectify those omissions through public statements and massive fund-raising from the celebrity-studded 46664 concerts.

ANC member Zackie Achmat's Treatment Action Campaign had become the most powerful lobby group on the issue.

Mbeki and other African leaders like Nigerian president Olusegun Obasanjo continued with their *sotto voce* approach to the rapacious Robert Mugabe.

On 5 May 2003, Nelson Mandela's law partner, fellow Robben Islander and long-time comrade-in-arms, Walter Sisulu, passed away.

Madiba's 85th birthday was marked by the opening of the Nelson Mandela Bridge between central Johannesburg and Braamfontein.

Deputy president Jacob Zuma, who was in charge of the Moral Regeneration Movement, was entangled in the fraud and corruption charges against his financial advisor Schabir Shaik.

The *Sunday Times* reported that former transport minister Mac Maharaj and his wife Zarina had received more than R500 000 from Schabir Shaik. Maharaj responded by publicly backing a *City Press* story, written by Zuma ally Ranjeni Munusamy, that National Prosecuting Authority head Bulelani Ngcuka was an apartheid-era spy. Maharaj's testimony at the subsequent Hefer Commission was discredited.

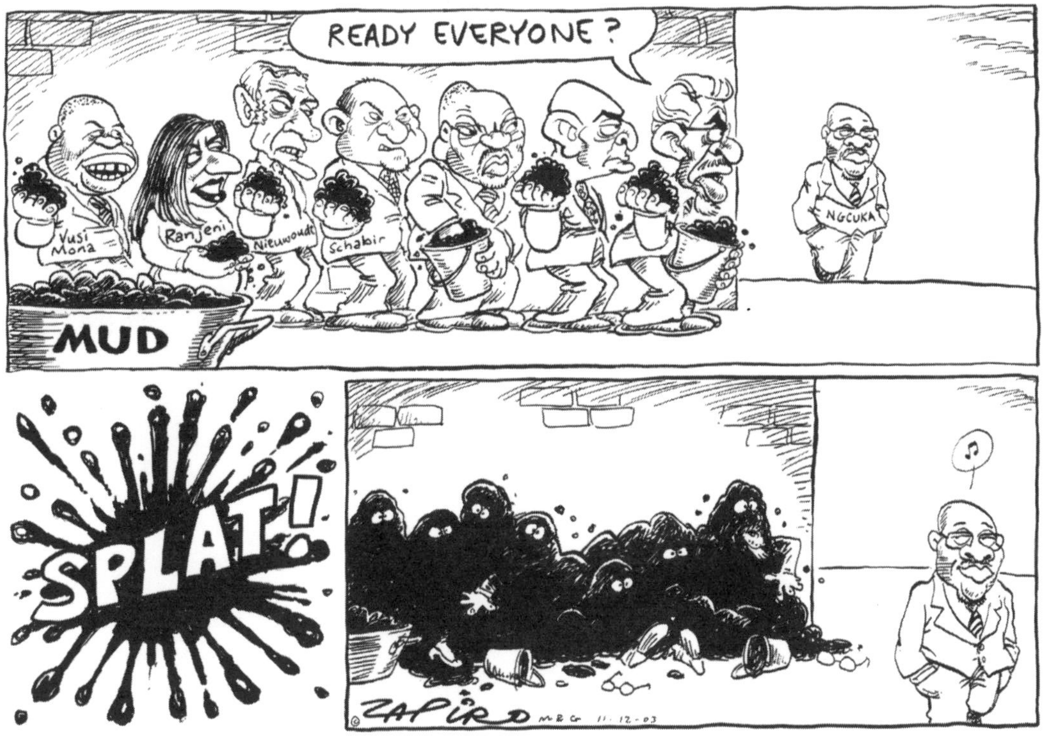
READY EVERYONE?
Vusi Mona
Ranjeni
Nieuwoudt
Schabir
NGCUKA
MUD
SPLAT!
ZAPIRO M&G 11-12-03

In a setback for Jacob Zuma and his allies, judge Hefer vindicated Bulelani Ngcuka.

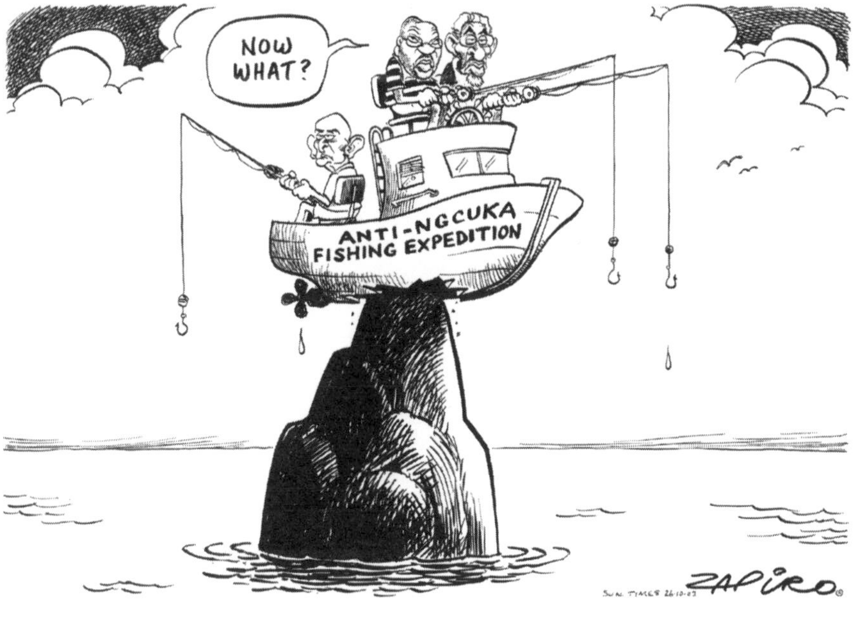
NOW WHAT?
ANTI-NGCUKA FISHING EXPEDITION
ZAPIRO

Safety and security minister Charles Nqakula was claiming success in the battle against crime.

The State of the
Nation Address
in February 2004
celebrated ten years
of democracy and
led into the third
election.

The ANC share of the vote increased by 3% to 69%. Archbishop Emeritus Desmond Tutu was critical of the lack of open debate on issues such as HIV/Aids in parliament.

After the election, the NNP formally disbanded and disappeared into the ANC. Leader Marthinus van Schalkwyk was rewarded with a cabinet post.

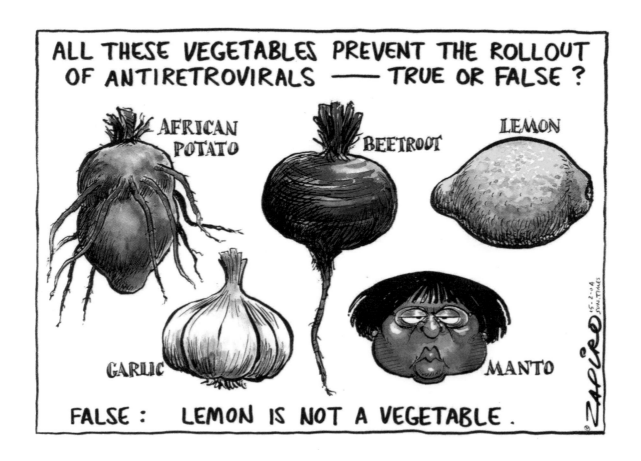

Health minister Manto Tshabalala-Msimang became known as Dr Beetroot for her promotion of vegetables over ARVs as a treatment for HIV/Aids.

In May 2004, Danny Jordaan and his bid team finally got the nod from Sepp Blatter and FIFA that they had deserved four years earlier.

Schabir Shaik was on trial in Durban because of his financial relationship with Jacob Zuma. If Shaik was to be found guilty of corruption, surely the deputy president would be next in court?

Nelson Mandela made a futile attempt to break free from burdensome public duties with his famous "don't call me, I'll call you" media conference.

Malusi Gigaba handed leadership of an increasingly bling and anti-communist ANC Youth League to Fikile Mbalula in August 2004.

Mbeki opened parliament in 2005 with the promised Better Life For All still a long way off and the institution itself deeply compromised by the Travelgate scandal involving the fraudulent use of travel vouchers by parliamentarians.

ANC chief whip Mbulelo Goniwe felt that it was the police probe that was harming the institution's reputation!

Wouter Basson, 'Dr Death' from the apartheid era, continued to defy the state's attempts to prosecute him.

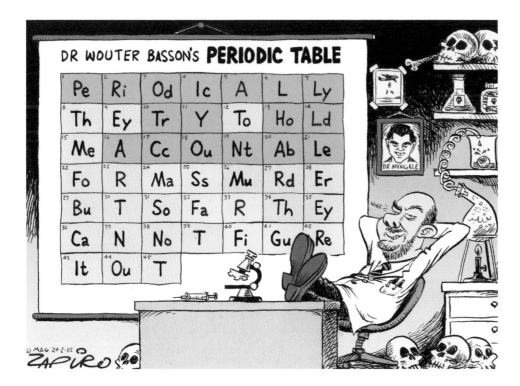

The 2005 Zimbabwean election was again characterised by ZANU-PF fraud and violence, which did not seem to greatly concern the SA observers or the president.

In June 2005, Schabir Shaik was found guilty of fraud and corruption. Judge Hilary Squires commented on the "mutually beneficial symbiosis" of Shaik's relationship with Zuma.

Two weeks after the verdict, Mbeki dismissed Zuma from the post of deputy president.

A powerful coalition of supporters formed around Zuma which included the prominent figures of COSATU secretary general Zwelinzima Vavi, ANC Youth League president Fikile Mbalula and SACP youth leader Buti Manamela.

CLASS OF 2005

Shaik received what was meant to be, effectively, a 15-year jail term but he spent much of his time in private medical care before an early release on medical grounds in 2009.

The 50th anniversary of the Freedom Charter, adopted on 26 June 1955.

On 27 September 2005, the controversial mining magnate and political party donor Brett Kebble was shot in a Johannesburg street. Kebble's business empire was collapsing and the killing was officially declared an assisted suicide. The ANC Youth League had been a particularly large recipient of Kebble's money.

Zuma's troubles deepened when he was charged with the rape of a 31-year-old daughter of a family friend who had been staying in his Johannesburg home and whom he knew to be HIV positive.

In November 2005, President
Mbeki inaugurated the Southern
African Large Telescope (SALT)
in the Karoo.

Manto Tshabalala-Msimang blamed the government's appalling record on the delivery of HIV/Aids treatment on pre-1994 inaction.

The State Opening of Parliament in 2006 took place amidst a plethora of scandals and an economy stubbornly reluctant to deliver.

The ANC's 2006 municipal election campaign involved an unhealthy compromise and uncharacteristic informality from Mbeki.

Eskom's supply failed to meet the nation's demands during the municipal elections.

A loose bolt reportedly caused the Koeberg power station to shut down, blacking out parts of the Western Cape. Public enterprises minister Alec Erwin blamed this on "sabotage", but the official report would later determine "negligence" as the cause.

Politics took a back seat for one glorious day when the Proteas successfully completed a world-record run chase against Australia in a one-day international at the Wanderers.

A prominent judge recused himself from the Zuma rape trial because the accused had fathered an illegitimate child with his sister. One of several such revelations.

During his evidence, Zuma said he had had consensual sex with the accused and admitted that he had not used a condom when having sex with the woman he knew was HIV positive. He told the court that he took a shower to try to reduce his risk of infection. Zuma was head of the National Aids Council at the time. Crowds of Zuma supporters gathered in the streets outside the court and Zuma often treated them to his signature struggle song.

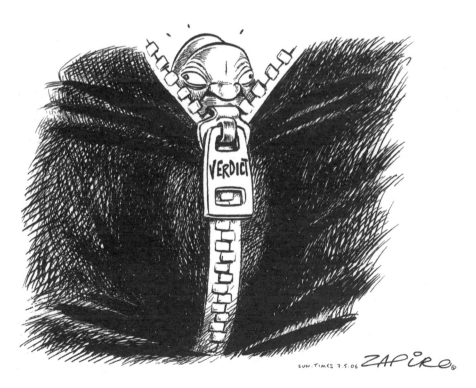

On 8 May 2006, judge Willem van der Merwe found Zuma not guilty, but was critical of his behaviour. The symbolic showerhead was about to become an iconic Zapiro fixture.

Jacob Zuma fired off the first of several big money lawsuits against Zapiro. After six years of intensive legal wrangling, none of them ever came to court.

The verdict revived Zuma's fraying political prospects and, with the backing of a powerful anti-Mbeki coalition, he became the dominant force in a bitter succession struggle which fractured the party and tested the diplomacy of secretary general Kgalema Motlanthe.

The leadership debate was often coded and laden with conspiracy theories. Zuma's supporters put forward the view that the rape charges against him were part of a plot to deprive him of the presidency.

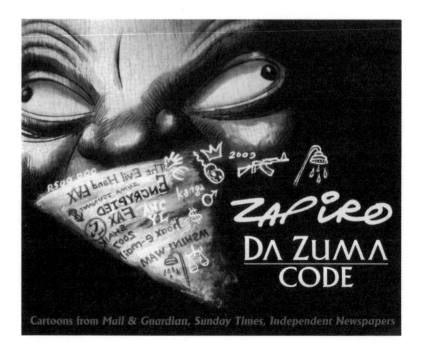

Zuma still faced the possibility of corruption and fraud charges and his supporters were increasingly concerned about the prospect of Cyril Ramaphosa entering the leadership fray.

Ramaphosa stayed out of the race and the nation was starting to come to terms with the bewildering likelihood that Jacob Zuma would be the next president.

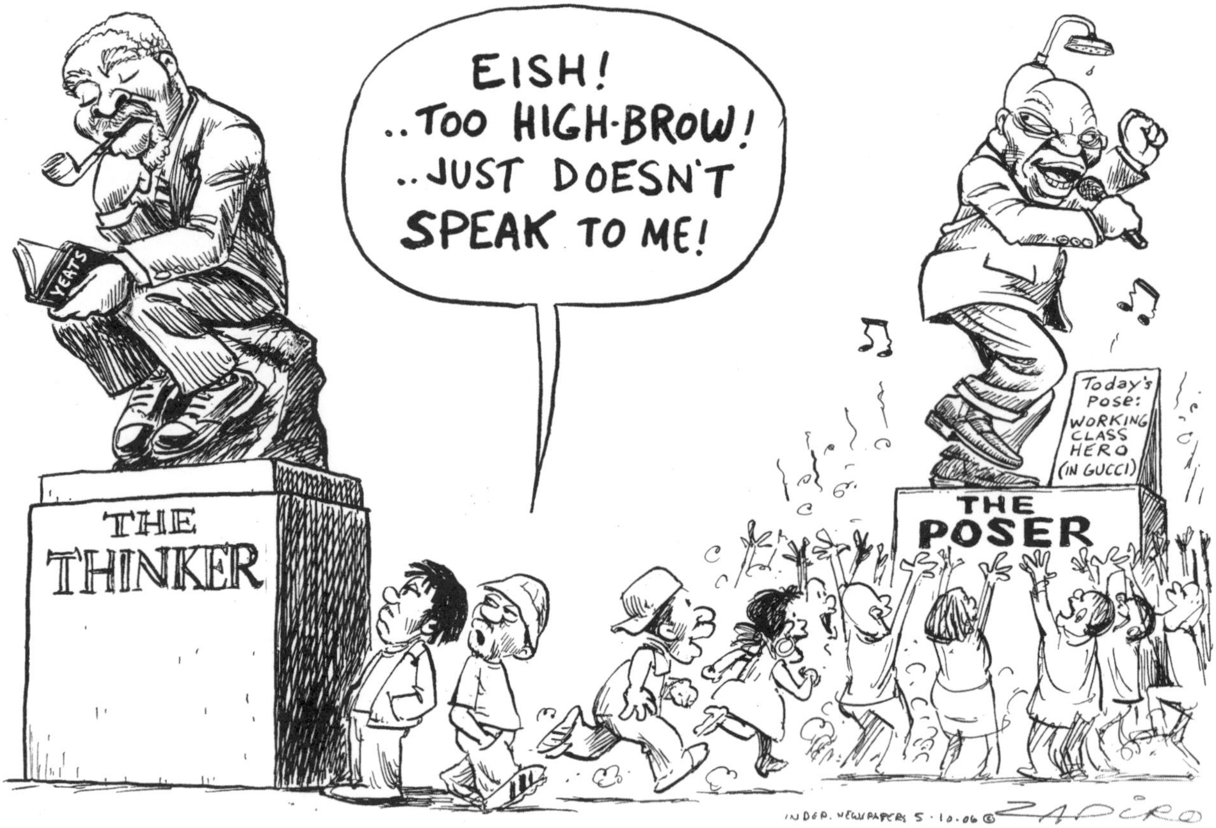
EISH! ..TOO HIGH-BROW! ..JUST DOESN'T SPEAK TO ME!
YEATS
THE THINKER
Today's Pose: WORKING CLASS HERO (IN GUCCI)
THE POSER
INDEP. NEWSPAPERS 5.10.06 © ZAPIRO

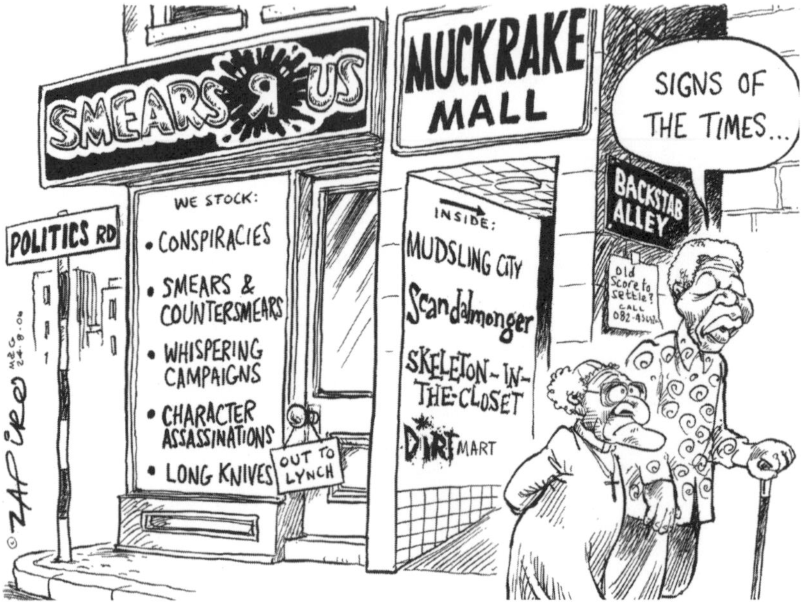
SMEARS R US
MUCKRAKE MALL
SIGNS OF THE TIMES...
BACKSTAB ALLEY
POLITICS RD
WE STOCK:
• CONSPIRACIES
• SMEARS & COUNTERSMEARS
• WHISPERING CAMPAIGNS
• CHARACTER ASSASSINATIONS
• LONG KNIVES
OUT TO LYNCH
INSIDE:
MUDSLING CITY
Scandalmonger
SKELETON-IN-THE-CLOSET
DIRT MART
Old Score to settle? CALL
© ZAPIRO M&G 24.8.06

THE NEW STRUGGLE

(concept reworked from 2001)
INDEP. NEWSPAPERS   15·6·06
©ZAPIRO

On HIV/Aids, Mbeki
and Tshabalala-Msimang
continued to defy
conventional medicine on
treatment programmes.

Corruption was never far from the headlines, especially with the Travelgate scandal rippling through parliament.

On 31 October 2006, PW
Botha died. Thabo Mbeki
attended the funeral and national
flags were flown at half-mast.

There were five schoolyard murders in eight months in 2006, but the fight against crime was hopelessly compromised by the serious allegations against the nation's top cop, Jackie Selebi.

Selebi's well-publicised connection to Glenn Agliotti, who was heavily implicated in the Kebble killing and other criminal activities, was starting to catch up with him, but the National Prosecuting Authority took out a court interdict gagging a *Mail & Guardian* exposé on the subject.

Selebi was president of the international policing body, Interpol, but would soon face a warrant of arrest for corruption, fraud, racketeering and defeating the ends of justice.

In November 2006, Tony Leon announced his intention to step down the following May as leader of the DA after eight years in charge.

Another senior policeman in trouble was Ekurhuleni Metro chief Robert McBride who was involved in a single-car collision after a Christmas party. Witnessess alleged he was under the influence of alcohol and he was charged with drunken driving, fraud and defeating the ends of justice. McBride produced a medical certificate stating that he was suffering from hypoglycaemia (low blood sugar), which it was alleged was fake.

Home affairs minister Nosiviwe Mapisa-Nqakula presided over a department so riddled with corruption and inefficiency that Britain moved to make visas compulsory for South African passport holders.

The increasingly rogue
behaviour of Robert Mugabe
produced no significant
change in policy from Pretoria.

It wasn't just events in Zimbabwe that were tarnishing Mbeki's dreams of a continental revival.

Deputy health minister Nozizwe Madlala-Routledge openly challenged the Aids denialism within government. She would be fired by Mbeki later in 2007.

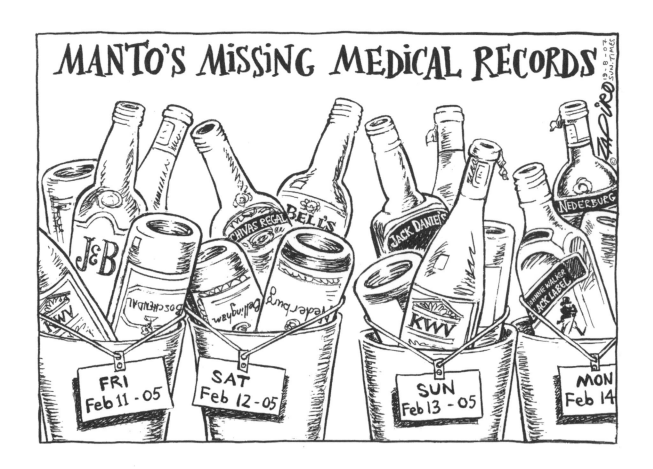

MANTO'S MISSING MEDICAL RECORDS

FRI
Feb 11 - 05

SAT
Feb 12-05

SUN
Feb 13 - 05

MON
Feb 14

In 2007 the health of the health minister became a major issue. The *Sunday Times* ran a controversial story about Tshabalala-Msimang's drinking habits during a hospital stay in 2005 that linked to her need for a liver transplant in 2007.

Cartoons from *Mail & Guardian, Sunday Times, Independent Newspapers*

Official bodies were dragging their feet on investigations into the Arms Deal, much to the frustration of Independent Democrats MP Patricia de Lille who had provided parliament with evidence of improper payments.

De Lille wasn't the only one targeting the corruption inherent in the deal – former ANC MP Andrew Feinstein and activist Terry Crawford-Browne both published damning books on the matter.

In May 2007, the mayor of Cape Town, Helen Zille, comfortably saw off the challenges of Joe Seremane and Athol Trollip to become the new leader of the DA.

Controversial Trinidadian writer Ronald Suresh Roberts produced a praise-singing biography of the increasingly authoritarian Mbeki.

Within the ANC the factional lines were being drawn ahead of the party's conference in Polokwane at the end of the year. The constitution barred Mbeki from a third term as president of the nation, but he sought to remain in charge of the party.

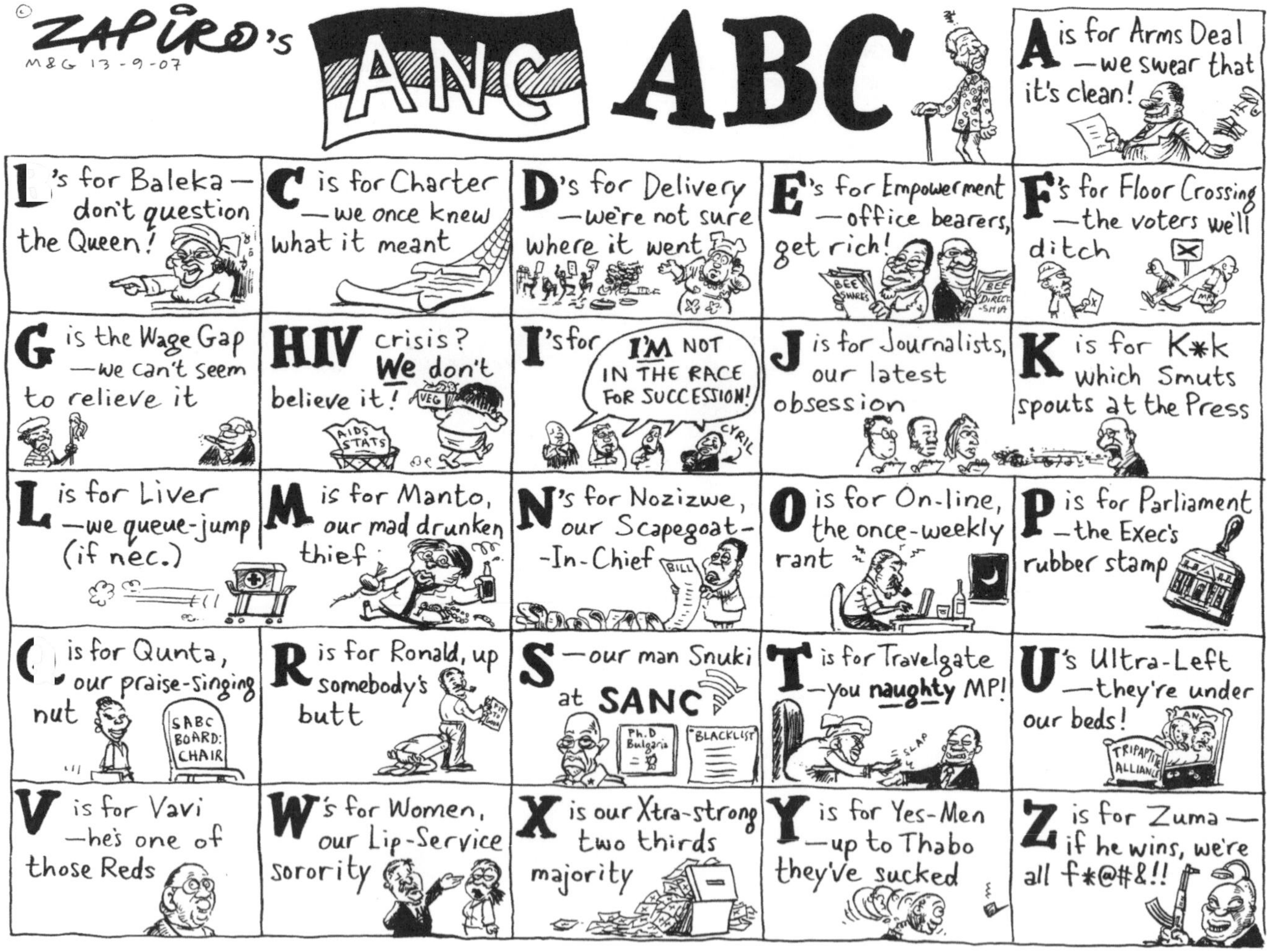
© ZAPIRO's
M&G 13-9-07
ANC ABC
A is for Arms Deal —we swear that it's clean!
L's for Baleka — don't question the Queen!
C is for Charter — we once knew what it meant
D's for Delivery — we're not sure where it went
E's for Empowerment — office bearers, get rich!
F's for Floor Crossing — the voters we'll ditch
MP
G is the Wage Gap — we can't seem to relieve it
HIV crisis? We don't believe it!
VEG
AIDS STATS
I's for
I'M NOT IN THE RACE FOR SUCCESSION!
CYRIL
J is for Journalists, our latest obsession
K is for K*k which Smuts spouts at the Press
L is for Liver — we queue-jump (if nec.)
M is for Manto, our mad drunken thief
N's for Nozizwe, our Scapegoat-In-Chief
BILL
O is for On-line, the once-weekly rant
P is for Parliament — the Exec's rubber stamp
Q is for Qunta, our praise-singing nut
SABC BOARD: CHAIR
R is for Ronald, up somebody's butt
S — our man Snuki at SANC
Ph.D Bulgaria
BLACKLIST
T is for Travelgate — you naughty MP!
SLAP
U's Ultra-Left — they're under our beds!
TRIPARTITE ALLIANCE
V is for Vavi — he's one of those Reds
W's for Women, our Lip-Service sorority
X is our Xtra-strong two thirds majority
Y is for Yes-Men — up to Thabo they've sucked
Z is for Zuma — if he wins, we're all f*@#&!!

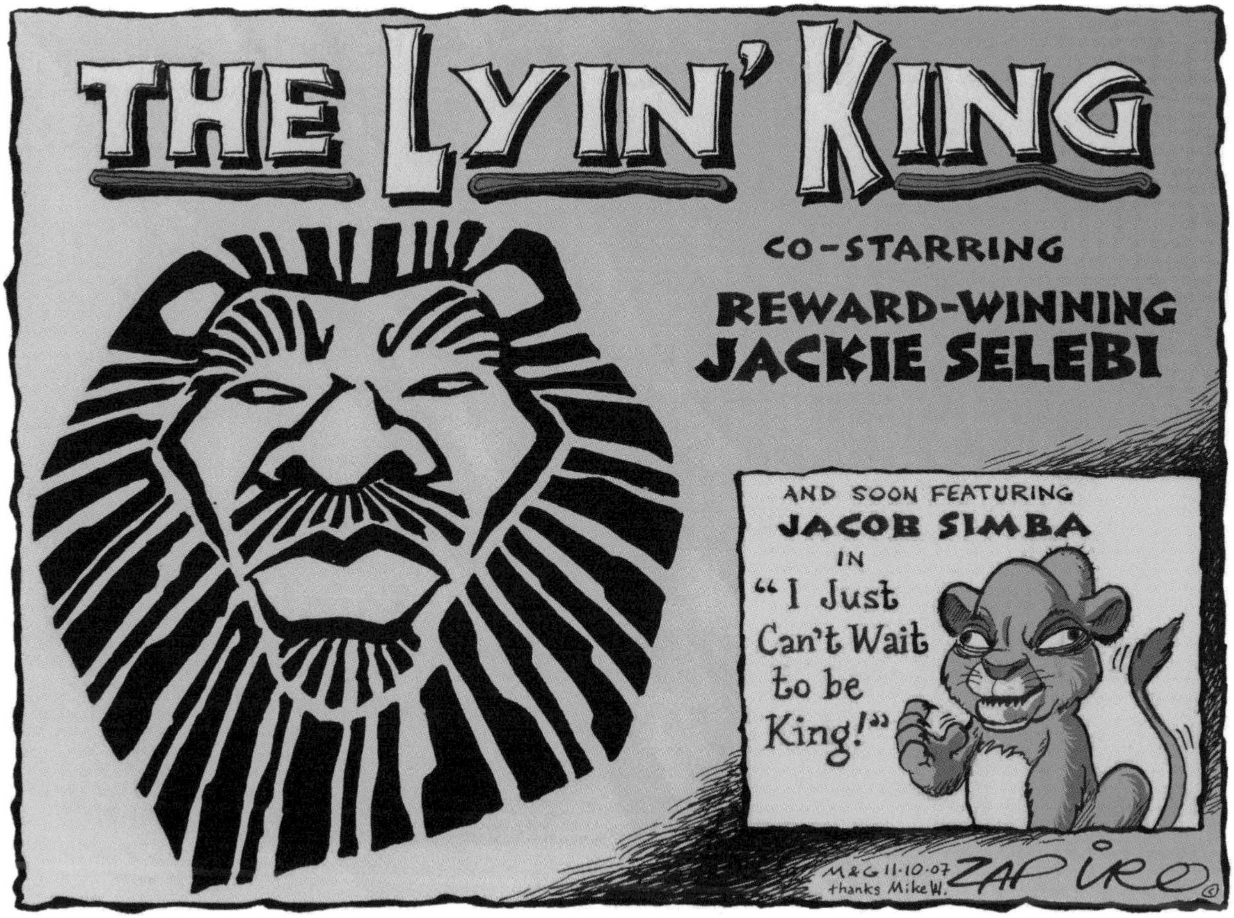
THE LYIN' KING
CO-STARRING
REWARD-WINNING
JACKIE SELEBI
AND SOON FEATURING
JACOB SIMBA
IN
"I Just Can't Wait to be King!"
M&G 11-10-07
thanks Mike W.
ZAPIRO

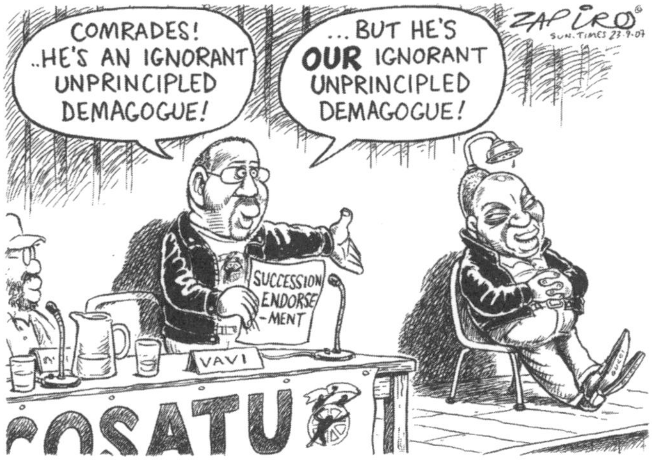
COMRADES! ..HE'S AN IGNORANT UNPRINCIPLED DEMAGOGUE!
...BUT HE'S OUR IGNORANT UNPRINCIPLED DEMAGOGUE!
ZAPIRO
SUN. TIMES 23-9-07
SUCCESSION ENDORSE-MENT
VAVI
COSATU

The triumph of Bryan Habana and the Springboks in the 2007 rugby world cup final provided some welcome, but only temporary, relief from the political turmoil on the road to Polokwane.

Acting NPA head Mokotedi Mpshe was still investigating the man who now had the support of five out of nine provincial party branches to be the next leader of the ANC.

Mbeki and his supporters had hopelessly misread the mood of the party and were completely routed in every ballot at a tempestuous and intolerant party conference which coincided with the latest round of Eskom load shedding. Zuma now ruled the party.

The outcome of Polokwane was a president in power yet without power.

Zuma's leftist backers soon discovered that the man they supported was happy to play all sides.

Zuma was not yet on the throne but he was now the controlling power behind it and set out, with the help of the party, to undermine the legal challenges against him. Safety and security minister Charles Nqakula confirmed that cabinet had begun the process of disbanding the Scorpions.

The Zimbabwean election in 2008 saw first-round results delayed for a month and the opposition MDC refusing to take part in a second ballot of what they called "a violent sham". The regional Southern African Development Community resolutely refused to act.

In May 2008, a series of
riots and attacks across
the country on resident
foreigners left a reported
40 people dead and
forcibly displaced many
thousands.

President Mbeki took a long time to respond to the outbreak of xenophobia. When he finally did comment he displayed a characteristic lack of emotional engagement.

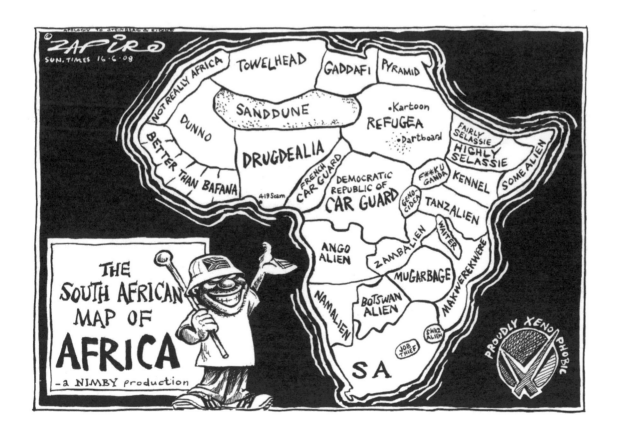

At 36, Fikile Mbalula had reached the official end of his shelf life as "a youth" and stood down as president of the ANCYL to be replaced in August 2008 by the new blustery force of South African politics, Julius Malema, under whose leadership the League pronounced it was "prepared to take up arms and kill for Zuma".

Minister in the presidency Essop Pahad and public enterprises minister Alec Erwin held a media briefing, which coincided with the Beijing Olympics, to deny allegations of corruption in the Arms Deal.

Zuma and his allies mounted a concerted campaign to gain control of every area of government, public institutions and state-connected business.

Zuma's tactics (and those of his supporters) included a determined effort to undermine the entire legal system unless charges against him were dropped or the courts ruled in his favour. ANC secretary general Gwede Mantashe described Constitutional Court judges as "counter-revolutionary". Zapiro's highly controversial take on this crisis provoked allegations of insensitivity from some critics, a Human Rights Council complaint from the Young Communist League (dismissed in 2010) and an, ultimately unfulfilled, lawsuit from Zuma for R7m.

In response to the cartoon, senior figures in the ANC affirmed that they did respect the constitutional independence of the judiciary.

The Pietermaritzburg High Court handed Zuma's
supporters the evidence they needed to remove Mbeki
from office when judge Chris Nicholson ruled that the
decision to prosecute Zuma on fraud and corruption
charges was procedurally invalid and found that claims
of "political undercurrents" in the process "were not
completely unbelievable". The inscrutable Mbeki
was recalled and replaced by Kgalema Motlanthe.
Nicholson's judgement was subsequently overturned
by the Supreme Court of Appeal.

Mbeki's recall sparked the first significant split in the
party of liberation, with Mosiuoa Lekota and Mbhazima
Shilowa leading the breakaway that became COPE
in the face of bitter criticism from Jeff Radebe and other
Zuma supporters.

2008-2009 THE MOTLANTHE YEAR

Kgalema Motlanthe began what everyone knew would
be a short term as a caretaker president with the difficult
task of restoring some confidence in the office after
a bitter internecine political conflict while, all the time,
knowing who was really in charge.

Suspended prosecutions head Vusi Pikoli was cleared by a commission of inquiry, but was still axed by President Motlanthe who also resisted calls for an Arms Deal inquiry.

The wild utterances of Julius Malema were increasingly dominating the political landscape without any apparent criticism from Zuma, a passivity he would later come to regret.

In February 2009 ANC spokesman Carl Niehaus stepped down after media reports of bad debts, broken promises and fraud.

NPA chief Mokotedi Mpshe and his deputy Willie Hofmeyr dropped the charges against Jacob Zuma after "intolerable abuse of process" allegedly revealed in a 2007 tape recording of former Scorpions boss Leonard McCarthy discussing the manipulation of the timing of the charges.

2009–2014 THE ZUMA YEARS

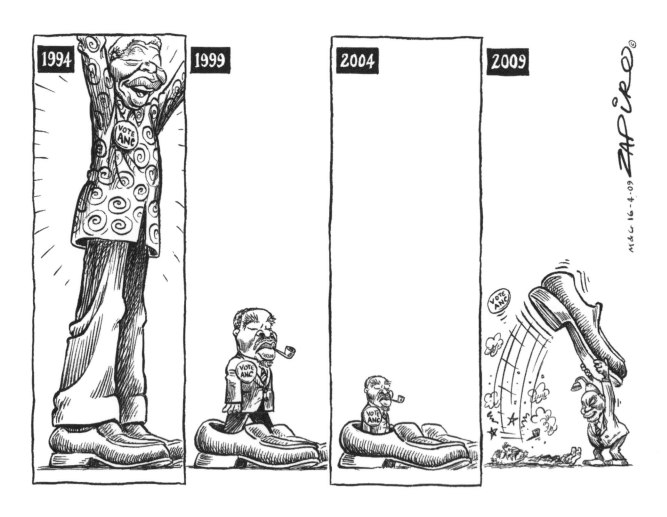

1994   1999   2004   2009

The 2009 election saw the ANC only marginally lose share – holding 65% of the vote – which meant that, in one of the most astonishing political survival acts of South African history, Jacob Gedleyihlekisa Zuma had emerged from years of personal and financial scandals as the nation's president.

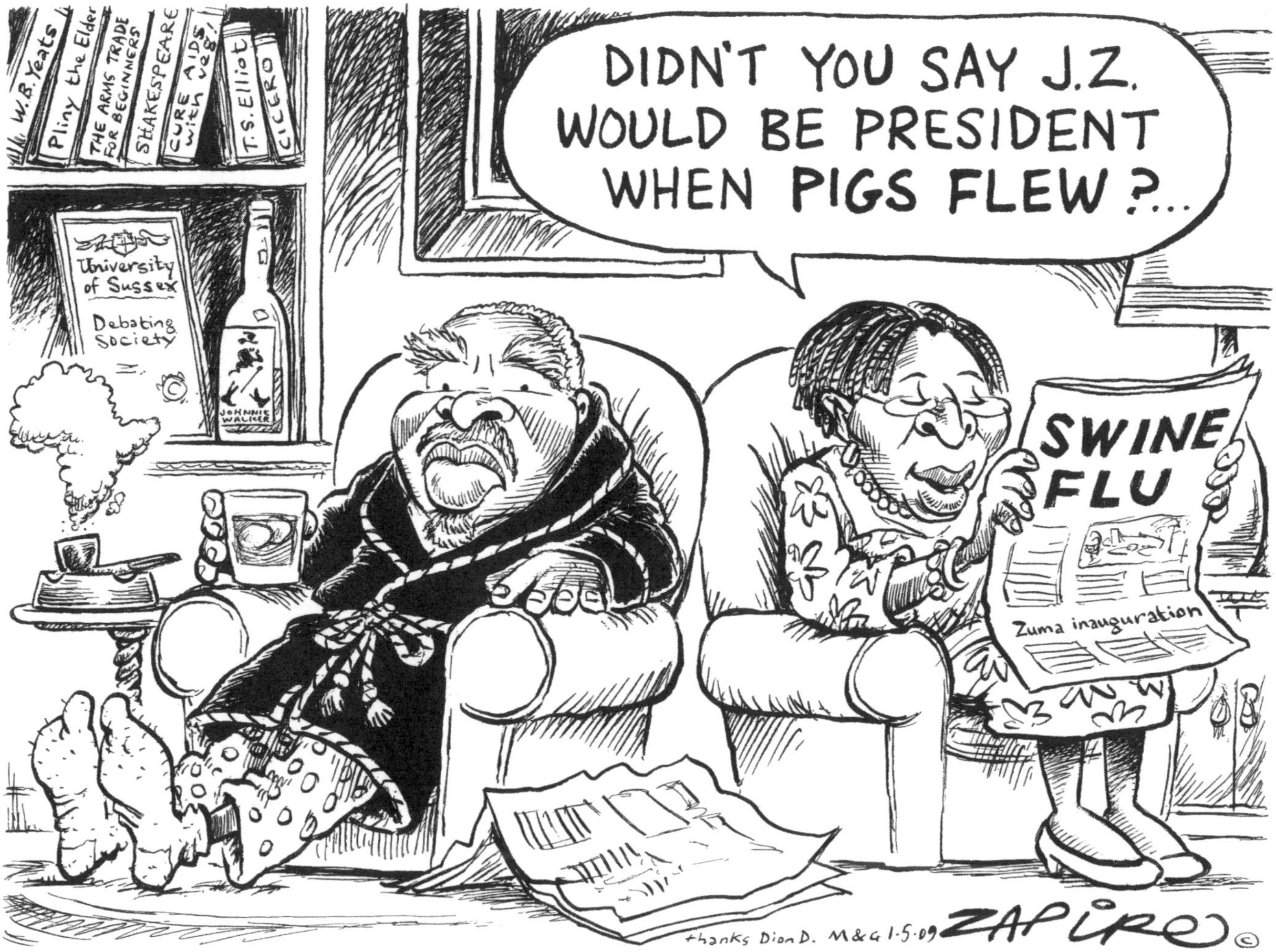
W.B.Yeats
Pliny the Elder
THE ARMS TRADE FOR BEGINNERS
SHAKESPEARE
CURE AIDS with veg!
T.S.Elliot
CICERO
University of Sussex
Debating Society
JOHNNIE WALKER
DIDN'T YOU SAY J.Z. WOULD BE PRESIDENT WHEN PIGS FLEW ?...
SWINE FLU
Zuma inauguration
thanks Dion D. M&G 1·5·09 ZAPIRO ©

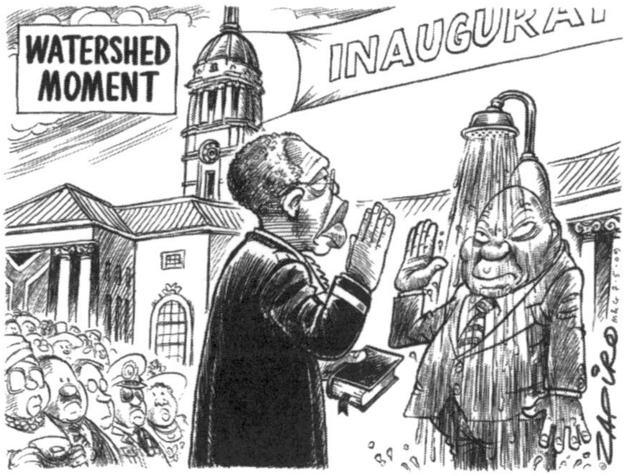
WATERSHED MOMENT
INAUGURAT
ZAPIRO

Zuma's first steps were positive, including a significant clearing out of some cabinet deadwood. Zapiro dabbled with removing the showerhead.

Transport minister Sbu Ndebele received a Mercedes and two cows from a contractor who benefited from government business. He asked Zuma what he should do.

Soon the political and economic realities were catching up on a president who seemed more comfortable dancing than governing.

Trevor Manuel's successor as finance minister, Pravin Gordhan, had a tough task on his hands.

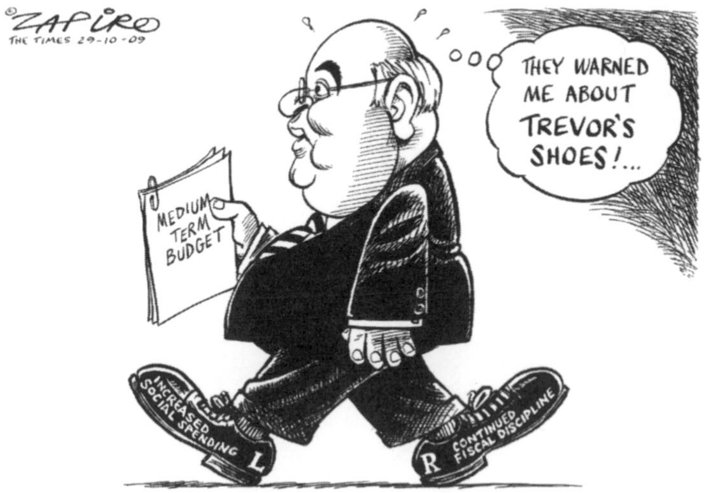
ZAPIRO
THE TIMES 29-10-09
THEY WARNED ME ABOUT TREVOR'S SHOES!...
MEDIUM TERM BUDGET
INCREASED SOCIAL SPENDING
L
R
CONTINUED FISCAL DISCIPLINE

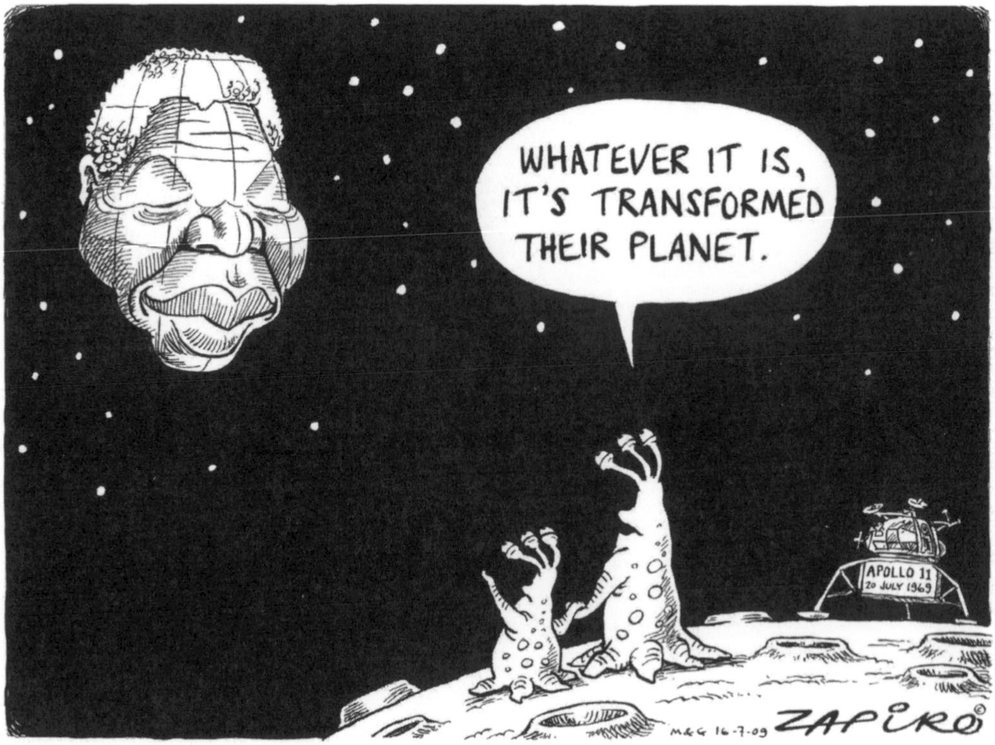
WHATEVER IT IS, IT'S TRANSFORMED THEIR PLANET.
APOLLO 11
20 JULY 1969
M&G 16-7-09 ZAPIRO

Nelson Mandela's 91st birthday.

Cape judge president John Hlophe's relentless and politicised defence against allegations of improperly influencing a Constitutional Court decision in favour of Jacob Zuma came close to causing a complete collapse in judicial administration.

Higher education minister and SACP boss Blade Nzimande got a R1.1m BMW as a perk of his job.

Zuma ally, lover of natty headgear and KZN MEC, Bheki Cele, became another political appointee at the head of the SAPS.

NEW POLICE MILITARY-STYLE RANKS

POLICING CAPABILITY

Cele was soon introducing military ranks and encouraging police to use deadly force.

Julius Malema's wild attacks on opponents and on alliance partners, especially the SACP, started to splinter the ANC.

The turbulence Zuma had created in the ANC to usurp Mbeki was becoming a permanent feature.

ANC veteran Kader Asmal said the party had "lost its moral compass" in its "use of intemperate language". He cited the Youth League's "kill for Zuma" and Fikile Mbalula's "shoot the bastards" comment about criminals.

THE SA HARDLINERS' PRESS STATEMENT FRIDGE MAGNET SET

WE WANT TO | CLARIFY | EMPHASIZE | DENY | OUR EARLIER STATEMENT REGARDING THE | TRAITOR | COMRADE | FORMER COMRADE | PROFESSOR WHO IS A | RACIST | IMPERIALIST | COCONUT | COUNTER-REVOLUTIONARY BABOON | RAVING LUNATIC | COCKROACH | WILD WHORE | GIGOLO BECAUSE WE | WERE MISQUOTED | OR IF YOU HAVE A RECORDING TAKEN OUT OF CONTEXT | AND NEVER | HARDLY EVER | SAID | HE | SHE SHOULD GO TO THE NEAREST CEMETERY | BE SHOT | IMPALED SCALPED | AND ANY | MEDIA LACKEY | MISCHIEF-MAKER | WHO CALLS THIS A RETRACTION | CLIMB-DOWN | ABOUT-TURN | IS A | BABOON | RACIST COCONUT | ETC.

ZAPIRO

SUN.TIMES 1-11-09
with apology to Tom Toles
for fridge magnet concept

The MK Military Veterans told Asmal to "go to the nearest cemetery and die". The Youth League wished a similar fate on UFS Rector Jonathan Jansen. Both organisations were constantly issuing apologies, corrections or clarifications for outrageous statements.

Barbara Hogan, after an impressive but short stint as health minister, was put in charge of a set of public enterprises that all seemed to be in leadership crises.

To general astonishment, the new head of the NPA was Menzi Simelane who had been discredited in the Ginwala inquiry into the suspension of former head Vusi Pikoli. Desmond Tutu called the appointment "an aberration" and the Constitutional Court would later rule it invalid.

At the start of 2010, the ANC was riven by Youth League plots to weaken senior figures on the left of the party.

11 February 2010 marked the 20th anniversary of Nelson Mandela's release from prison.

Baby Shower

Jacob Zuma had just married his third wife and had another fiancée, when, prior to his 2010 State of the Nation Address, news broke of his child out of wedlock with the 39-year-old daughter of soccer boss Irvin Khoza.

Zapiro's showerhead was back with a vengeance.

The 2010 State of the Nation Address was short on substance.

Cavalcades of expensive vehicles accompanied by aggressive security personnel increasingly came to symbolise ANC administration both nationally and provincially. A UCT student was arrested after allegedly showing a finger to the president's blue-light convoy.

In March 2010
President Zuma paid
a state visit to Britain.

On 3 April 2010, AWB founder and leader Eugène Terre'Blanche was murdered in his home by farm workers amid controversy over the singing of "Shoot the Boer" ("Dubul' ibhunu") by Julius Malema.

In a classic Zuma fudge, left-leaning economic development minister Ebrahim Patel's Economic Advisory Panel and the more centrist Trevor Manuel's National Planning Commission were left to battle it out over the fiscal future.

The DA administration in the Cape installed open toilets in Khayelitsha and left residents to add the walls. The Human Rights Commission found that the city had "violated the rights" of the users.

While the economy failed to deliver broad-based benefits, the nation defied many sceptics and delivered a remarkably successful soccer world cup during a period in which the country was, in many ways, actually governed by the all-powerful FIFA president Sepp Blatter.

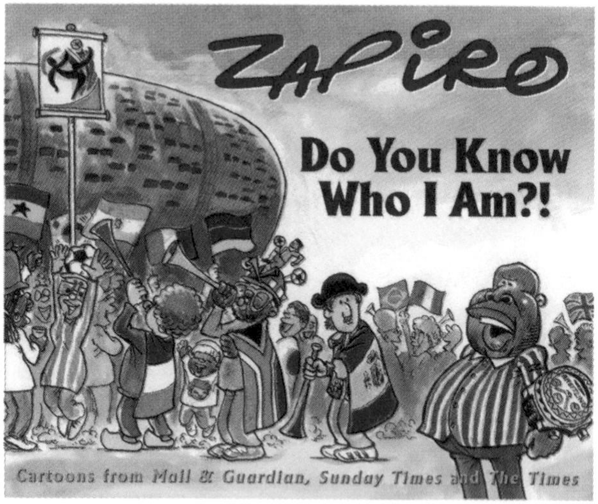
ZAPIRO
Do You Know Who I Am?!
Cartoons from Mail & Guardian, Sunday Times and The Times

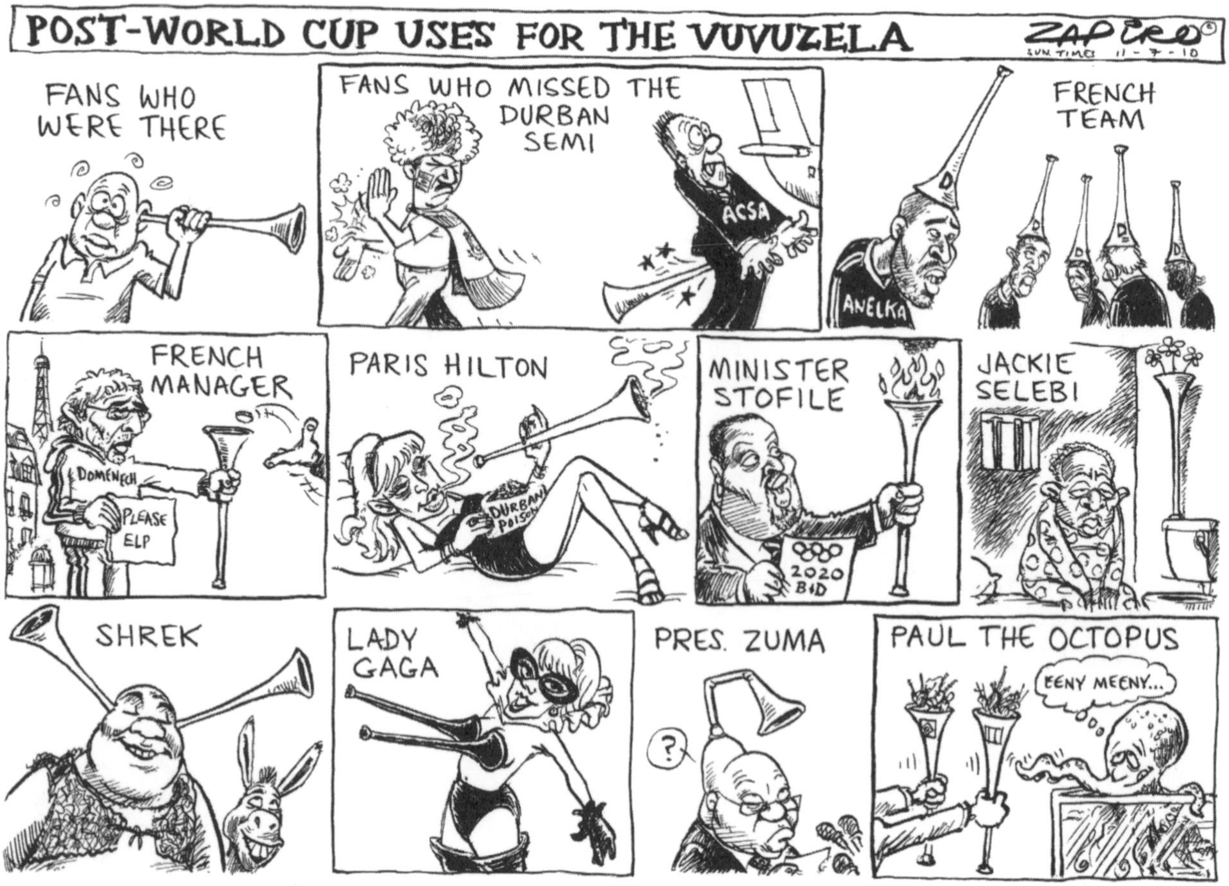
POST-WORLD CUP USES FOR THE VUVUZELA
ZAPIRO©
SUN. TIMES 11-7-10
FANS WHO WERE THERE
FANS WHO MISSED THE DURBAN SEMI
ACSA
FRENCH TEAM
ANELKA
FRENCH MANAGER
DOMENECH
PLEASE ELP
PARIS HILTON
DURBAN POISON
MINISTER STOFILE
2020 BID
JACKIE SELEBI
SHREK
LADY GAGA
PRES. ZUMA
?
PAUL THE OCTOPUS
EENY MEENY...

The disbanded Scorpions had been replaced by the Directorate for Priority Crime Investigation (the Hawks), which shut down the existing Scorpions' Arms Deal inquiries.

The once-promising COPE, which had attracted 7% of the vote in the 2009 election, was destroying itself through the bitter battle between leaders Mosiuoa Lekota, Mbhazima Shilowa and Mvume Dandala.

The government's Broad-Based Black Economic Empowerment (BBBEE) policy was facing criticism for its narrow base of beneficiaries. The president's nephew Khulubuse was growing richer and wider while workers at his Aurora mines went unpaid.

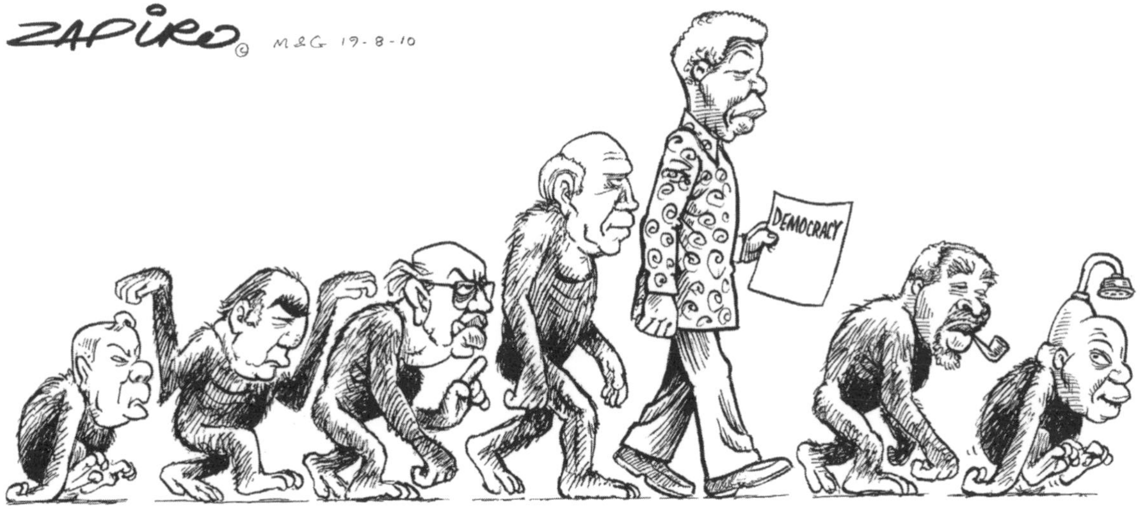
ZAPIRO© M&G 19-8-10
DEMOCRACY

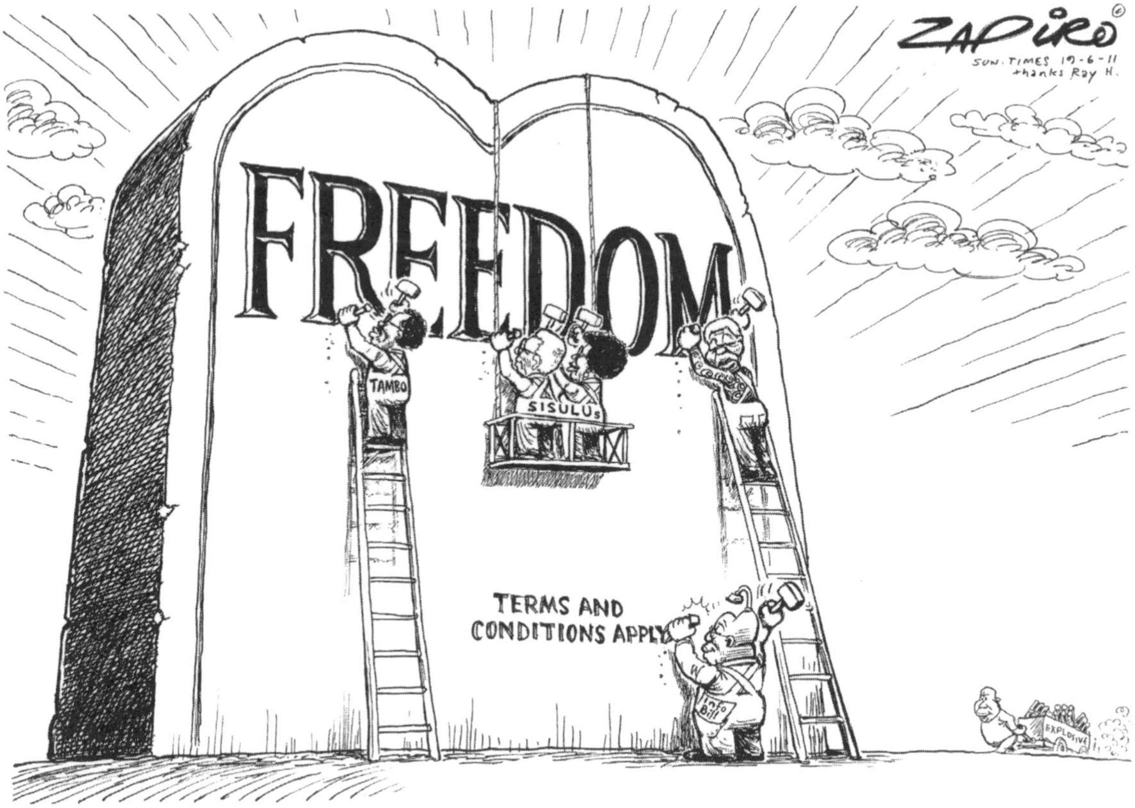
ZAPIRO©
SUN. TIMES 19-6-11
thanks Ray H.
FREEDOM
TAMBO
SISULUs
TERMS AND
CONDITIONS APPLY
Info Bill
EXPLOSIVE

ANC senior structures finally lost patience with Julius Malema and charged him with a string of offences – a verbal attack on a BBC journalist, unfavourably comparing Zuma to Mugabe and his singing of "Shoot the Boer" after it was banned. After plea-bargaining, the party demanded a public apology for his conduct, fined him R10 000 and ordered him to attend anger management classes.

Heading up to the ANC's National General Council (NGC) meeting in Durban, Zuma's future as leader was being openly questioned.

At the NGC, the party found a convenient way to unite all factions by attacking the media, with SACP boss Blade Nzimande leading the calls for a media tribunal to "hold journalists accountable".

COSATU secretary-general Zwelinzima Vavi, once a passionate supporter of Zuma, was becoming increasingly critical of the government, saying that "we're headed for a predator state where a powerful, corrupt and demagogic elite of political hyenas are increasingly using the state to get rich".

The Sushi King – Kenny Kunene – symbolised the bling of the new elite with his outrageous parties, which occasionally involved his favourite food being consumed off the bodies of naked models.

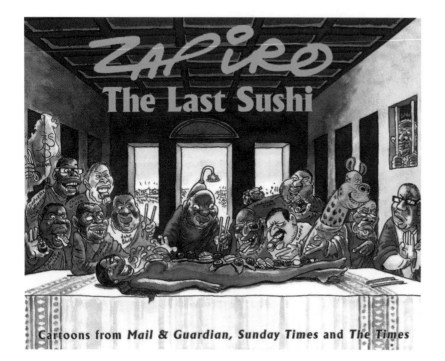

184

State of the Nation Address 2011 – Zuma in 2010 had grandiosely promised a year of action on jobs and delivery.

During campaigning for the 2011 municipal elections, Jacob Zuma was reported as saying that to vote for the ANC was "to choose heaven", while a vote for the opposition amounted to "choosing hell".

ZAPIRO SUN. TIMES 10-4-11

During the same campaign Julius Malema told his audience in the Eastern Cape, "President Mandela is sick and you don't want to contribute to a worsening condition of Mandela by not voting ANC. President Mandela will never endure if the ANC is out of power."

The office of Public Protector had been occupied without particular distinction until President Zuma appointed advocate Thuli Madonsela. Her investigation into an unlawfully authorised SAPS office lease in Pretoria marked her as an independent force. She damned the actions of police commissioner Bheki Cele and public works minister Gwen Mahlangu-Nkabinde in the awarding of the R500m lease to Roux Shabangu, a friend of Jacob Zuma.

THE TIMES 10-3-11

While Cele proclaimed his innocence, the crime intelligence unit launched an "unauthorised" raid on Madonsela's offices. Cele insisted that the report was legally and factually flawed but Zuma dismissed him nonetheless.

Government relationships with the media took a turn for the worse with the extraordinary decision to appoint the confrontational and controversial Jimmy Manyi as its primary spokesperson.

The infamous *Ministerial Handbook* seemed to cover every exorbitant piece of official expenditure, including the hundreds of thousands of rands the minister of co-operative governance and traditional affairs, Sicelo Shiceka, reportedly spent on luxury hotels, first-class air tickets and visiting a jailed girlfriend in Switzerland.

Zwelinzima Vavi again criticised the ANC commenting that, "politics are dying. Individualism and greed are on the rise".

The row over open toilets in the Western Cape and in the Free State became the main issue of the 2011 municipal elections.

The elections saw the ANC lose votes in every province except KZN and the DA vote grow markedly.

Two struggle icons, Albertina
Sisulu and Kader Asmal,
passed away in June 2011.

Acting on the advice of his lawyers, President Zuma unilaterally extended the term of chief justice Sandile Ngcobo in a way that was ruled unconstitutional because such an extension could only be granted by an Act of Parliament.

As a replacement for Ngcobo, Zuma, to general bewilderment in legal circles, appointed the inexperienced and conservative former homelands' judge Mogoeng Mogoeng instead of promoting the obvious candidate, deputy chief justice Dikgang Moseneke.

ZANU-PF's expropriation without compensation land reform programme had virtually destroyed Zimbabwe's economy yet Julius Malema was calling for a similar approach in South Africa.

Malema's sidekick and spokesman Floyd Shivambu had a unique way of dealing with the media.

Malema's extravagant lifestyle and opaque source of finances were attracting the attention of several investigative branches of the state.

In August 2011, the ANC's National Disciplinary Committee met to consider charges against Malema, including his call for the overthrow of the Botswanan government. A rally of his supporters in the centre of Johannesburg turned violent and Malema, adopting a Zuma-like legal strategy, challenged every part of the party's procedures.

When Swedish company SAAB formally admitted that it had paid R24 million in bribes to clinch its part in the Arms Deal, Hawks' boss Anwa Dramat felt obligated to reopen his investigation.

Zuma finally announced a government inquiry into the Arms Deal to be headed by judge Willie Seriti just ahead of the finalisation of a Constitutional Court action from activist Terry Crawford-Browne that would have forced him to do so anyway.

Zuma's spokesman Mac Maharaj laid criminal charges
against the *Mail & Guardian* to prevent publication
of allegations against him and his wife that they had
received money from Schabir Shaik in connection
with two multimillion-rand contracts awarded by the
department of transport whilst Maharaj was minister.

In November Malema
was suspended from the
ANC for five years.

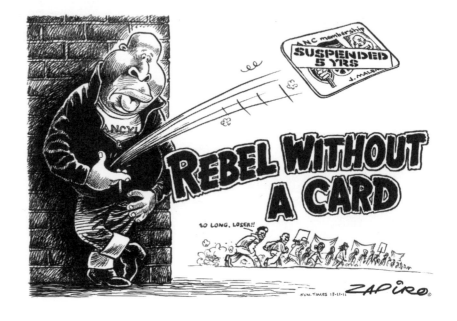

Education minister Angie Motshekga met with considerable scepticism when she claimed success with improved matric pass rates.

The non-delivery of text books in Limpopo was a running sore for her department.

Mass protests took place on "Black Tuesday" as the controversial Protection of Information Bill (AKA the Secrecy Bill) was put to a vote in parliament.

On 8 January 2012, the ANC celebrated its past but everyone in the party was fighting for its future, which would be determined at the Mangaung conference in December.

The big guns in the developing economy world invited South Africa to the BRICS party.

Early in 2012, the government hit full-blown resistance from within the Alliance to the e-tolling of Gauteng's freeways and responded with characteristic indecision.

Julius Malema lost his final appeal and was formally expelled from the ANC. He was soon extolling the virtues of former president Thabo Mbeki, a man Malema had played a key role in driving from office.

A senior court ordered the NPA to give the DA access to records of material considered when charges against Zuma had been dropped in 2009.

Crime intelligence boss Richard Mdluli was reported to be a Zuma ally. A series of serious charges against him and investigations into his behaviour were all either dropped or postponed.

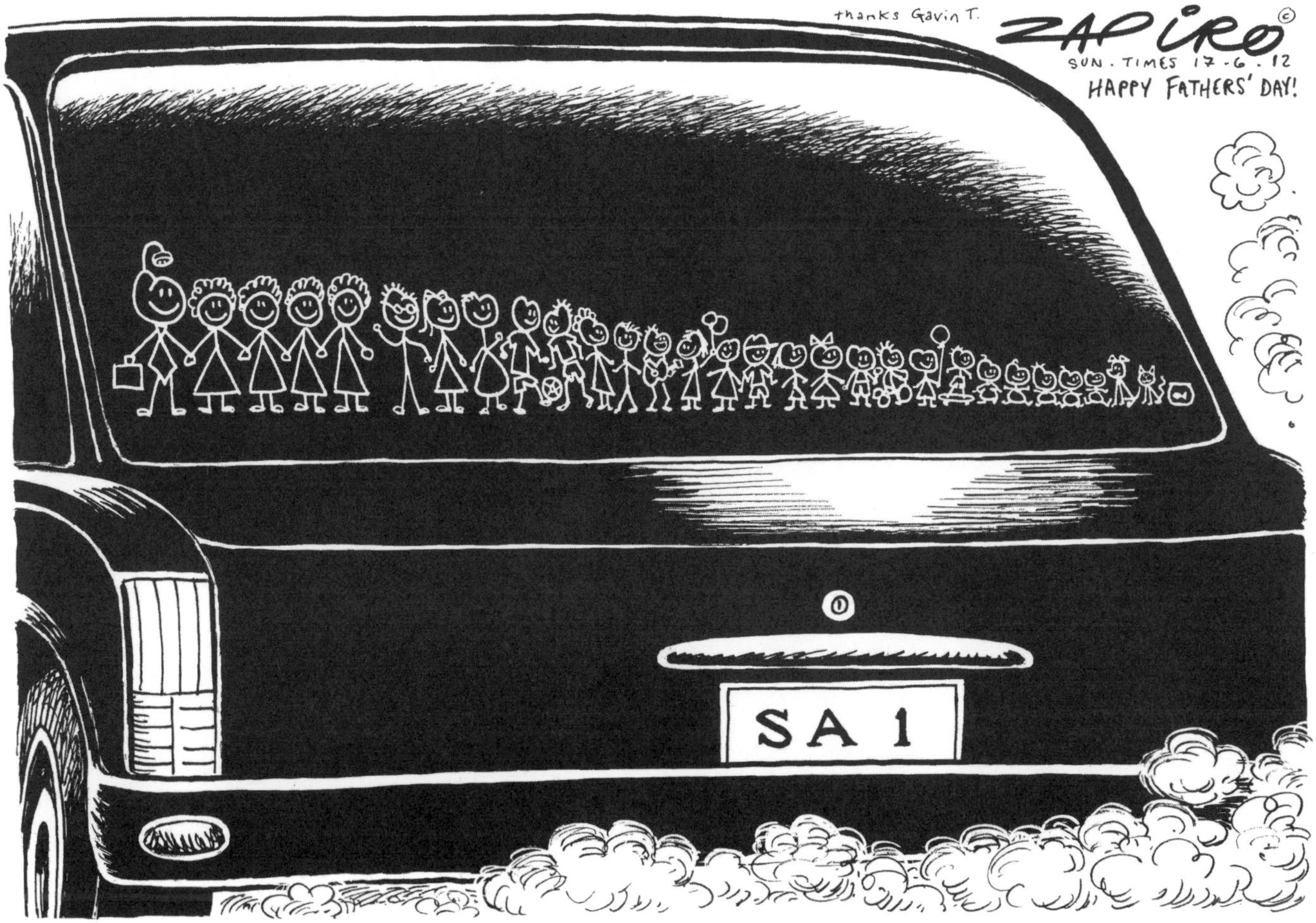
thanks Gavin T.
ZAPIRO©
SUN. TIMES 17-6-12
HAPPY FATHERS' DAY!
SA 1

Father's Day 2012.

Artist Brett Murray exhibited a painting in a Johannesburg gallery of President Jacob Zuma with his genitals exposed, entitled *The Spear*. The ANC responded furiously with a defamation suit and actions to force the gallery and the website of *City Press* (edited by Ferial Haffajee) to remove all evidence of the painting. When they both agreed, ANC secretary general Gwede Mantashe declared "Mission accomplished, comrades".

©ZAPIRO
M&G 31-5-12
MISSION ACCOMPLISHED!
FREEDOM OF EXPRESSION
GOODMAN GALLERY
City Press
Ferial H
Brett M
S.S.STALIN
The Doors of Learning and Culture Shall Be Opened to Conformist Lackeys

ZAPIRO
But Will It Stand Up In Court?
Cartoons from Mail & Guardian, Sunday Times and The Times

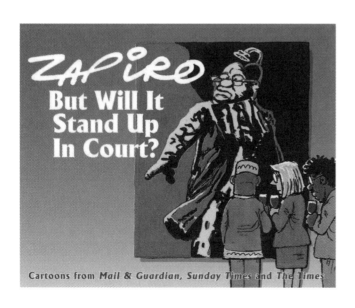

In the Byzantine and undeclared party leadership contest between Zuma and Kgalema Motlanthe, immense significance was placed in ANC economic policy debates on whether South Africa was entering the "second transition" or the "second phase of the transition".

The London Olympics made local heroes Chad le Clos and Oscar Pistorius global superstars.

On 16 August 2012, in the most lethal use of force by South African security forces since Sharpeville more than 50 years earlier, the SAPS killed 34 striking mineworkers at Marikana and wounded over 70.

Julius Malema immediately made his presence felt on the ground at Marikana, aligning himself with the newly formed Association of Mineworkers and Construction Union (AMCU) and against the government, COSATU and business.

President Zuma announced a commission of inquiry into the Marikana shootings, to be headed by judge Ian Farlam.

In the wake of Marikana, violent protests about the lack of service delivery spread across the country. The ANC seemed more concerned about Mangaung.

After four years of threats and just as the case was due to come to court, President Zuma withdrew all claims for damages against Zapiro for the Lady Justice cartoon and agreed to pay half of his and the newspaper's costs.

Possible ANC leadership candidate and director of Marikana mining company Lonmin, Cyril Ramaphosa, was embarassed by revelations of an exorbitant auction bid which he had made for a single buffalo bull for his game farm.

The Public Protector was starting her investigation into the exorbitant spending on Zuma's private residence at Nkandla. The government was claiming it was a National Key Point and therefore subject to official secrecy.

President Zuma made a claim in parliament that he had taken out a bond to cover his private costs at Nkandla but he never advanced any evidence of the loan.

A bitter and occasionally violent strike by wine and fruit farmworkers in the Western Cape for a rise in wages and better working conditions coincided with Bafana Bafana coach Gordon Igesund's desperate search for a goalscorer at the African Cup of Nations.

In the run-up to Mangaung, the names of Kgalema Motlanthe and Cyril Ramaphosa loomed large as potential leadership figures, but neither openly declared candidacies nor advanced any definitive policy positions.

Zuma comfortably saw off Motlanthe's belated official challenge for the party presidency and billionaire businessman Ramaphosa became his deputy.

Public works minister Thulas Nxesi claimed that a "classified" inter-ministerial report exonerated Zuma on the Nkandla issue. Expenditure on the "security upgrades" had ballooned from the original estimate of R27m to well over R200m.

On Valentine's Day
2013, Oscar Pistorius
killed his girlfriend Reeva
Steenkamp. The media
world became fixated on
this spectacular fall from
a pedestal.

The police investigation of the Pistorius case was severely criticised, but the SAPS was facing far more serious issues around repeated brutality, which reached a peak when taxi-driver Mido Macia was dragged through Daveyton strapped to the back of an SAPS van and later died in custody.

President Zuma was hosting the BRICS Summit in Durban when 13 SANDF members were killed while futilely defending the dictatorial government in the Central African Republic (CAR).

Rumours abounded on the health of Nelson Mandela. He clung to life while the nation feared for the worst.

Some of Mandela's family members shamed his name with squabbling and publicity-seeking antics.

The reputation of the National Prosecuting Authority (NPA) was in tatters after a series of completely botched high-profile cases, including the failed attempt to make highly controversial disciplinary charges stick against one of their own best prosecutors, Glynnis Breytenbach.

On the eve of Freedom Day 2013, Parliament passed the Protection of State Information Bill, which increased the government's power to restrict access to information and to impose hefty fines and jail terms on reporters who publish classified information.

Zwelinzima Vavi was accused of rape by a colleague who claimed he had offered her a job at COSATU without following proper recruitment procedures. Vavi's opponents within the union movement and the ANC took the opportunity to suspend and discipline him. Vavi admitted to having consensual sex with the woman who later withdrew the rape charge.

The Gupta brothers – Rajesh, Ajay and Atul – were a pervasive presence as they lavished attention, money, employment and business opportunities on Jacob Zuma and members of his family. Government contracts came their way and their newspaper, *The New Age*, benefited from disproportionate state advertising.

The Guptas overplayed their hand when they requested, and received, unprecedented permission to use the SANDF's Waterkloof airforce base to land a private plane carrying guests to a family wedding in Sun City. A police escort was also provided.

The government's report on the scandal from justice minister Jeff Radebe fingered only hapless officials who apparently acted on the assumption that Zuma, described in evidence as "Number One", had approved the landing without ever checking if this was the case.

Julius Malema (with Floyd Shivambu's help) was trying to drum up support for his new Economic Freedom Fighters while, at the same time, dealing with charges of fraud and money laundering, and SARS claims that he owed them R16m.

The always fractious politics of the Western Cape reached a new low when faeces became a medium of protest. Human waste was dumped on the steps of the provincial legislature and thrown around Cape Town International Airport.

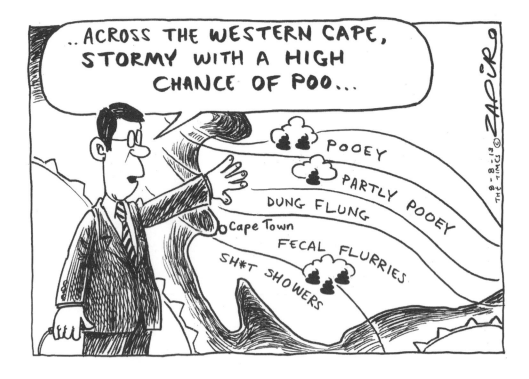

As usual, the annual crime statistics sparked disagreement. General Phiyega and the government hailed the long-term downward trend in murder, while critics pointed to a year-on-year increase and the appalling track record of the SAPS in the previous 12 months.

Parliament's Ethics Committee, headed by ANC veteran Ben Turok, found that former communications minister Dina Pule, who had an infamously expensive taste in shoes, had "wilfully misled" parliament and breached the code of conduct for MPs. Pule, whose time in office inluded some disastrous mismanagement of the SABC, had provided improper benefits to her partner Phosane Mngqibisa while denying the relationship.

After a long period of indecision and court actions, the government pressed ahead with the implementation of the deeply unpopular e-tolling system in Gauteng.

Dr Mamphela Ramphele had been a persistent thorn in the side of the ANC as an authoritative voice in civil society. In June 2013 she announced her seemingly ill-defined intention to enter politics.

The High Court ordered the NPA to hand over to the DA the alleged "Spy Tapes", which were used by the NPA in 2009 as the basis for the dropping of corruption charges against Jacob Zuma. The NPA and Zuma's legal team continued to resist the court's demands.

The DA changed its mind on the approval of black empowerment legislation. The costly flip-flop caused divisions in the party and a rift between Helen Zille and parliamentary leader Lindiwe Mazibuko.

Capetonian Nick Sloane
was in charge of the
astonishing salvage
operation of the cruise liner
Costa Concordia, which
was wrecked off the coast
of Italy in January 2012.

Speaking in a Limpopo church, Zuma gave his spin doctor Mac Maharaj yet another challenge when he claimed that, "God has made a connection between the government and the church. That's why he says you, as a church, should pray for it."

The state's attempts to justify the "security measures" at Nkandla reached farcical levels when the new swimming pool was described as "a fire pool" for emergency use.

Public Protector Thuli Madonsela persisted with her investigation into the Nkandla expenditure in the face of obstruction, obfuscation and legal challenges from security cluster ministers.

THE HOUSE THAT JACOB BUILT

ZAPIRO
SUN. TIMES 24-11-13

SECURITY CLUSTER

THESE ARE THE STOOGES ALL PUFFED UP
WHO'LL NEVER ADMIT HOW THEY STUFFED UP
SPENDING MILLIONS OF TAXPAYERS' MONEY
AND THEN MAKING UP STORIES (HELLUVA FUNNY!)
DEFENDING EXTRAVAGANT BITS AND PIECES
FOR **JACOB** AND WIVES, KIDS, NEPHEWS AND NIECES.
RONDAWELS AND HOUSES OF VARYING SIZE
WERE PAID FOR BY JACOB (HMMM!..THIS SOUNDS LIKE LIES)
THE PUBLIC (THEY SAY) IS JUST FOOTING THE BILL
FOR **SECURITY FEATURES** — ONLY **200 MIL!**
THE FENCES AND GATES KEEP OUT '**LOCAL MARAUDERS'**
(WE WISH THEY HAD SAFEGUARDS AGAINST **TENDER FRAUDERS**)
FOR SECURITY GUARDS THERE ARE **TWO SOCCER PITCHES**
AND LASERS WITH BACKUP IN CASE THERE ARE GLITCHES
THERE'S PROTECTION FROM **EARTHQUAKES** (WHICH NEVER OCCUR)
AND DITTO FOR **FLOODS** ('COS IT'S BEST TO BE SURE?)
THERE ARE **TWO HELIPADS** AND ROADS THAT THEY'LL WIDEN
AND A **NEW CHICKEN COOP** THAT IS HARDER TO HIDE IN (!!)
THEY'VE SECURED JACOB'S SAFETY IN EVERY WHICH SECTOR
— EXCEPT **NOBODY'S** SAFE FROM THE **PUBLIC PROTECTOR!**

SO THIS IS THE HOUSE THAT **JACOB** BUILT
... AND SO DID **YOU** AND SO DID **I**
AND SO DID **SIPHO** AND **PENNY** AND **TY**
AND **VUYO** AND **HANIEF** AND **THANDI** AND **JULIE**
AND **FANIE** AND **MANNY** AND **ABDUL** AND **THULI**
THIS IS THE HOUSE THAT **ALL** OF US PAID FOR
BUT IT'S ONLY **JACOB** WHOM IT WAS MADE FOR!
..WHICH IS WHY YOU'RE IRATE THAT IF YOU TAKE A **PICTURE**
THOSE HIGH-HANDED STOOGES HAVE VOWED TO CONVICT YA!

NO PHOTOS!

A SELFIE AT NKANDLA? ..ME TOO!

Parliament's Joint Standing Committee on Intelligence tabled a report detailing the reasons for over R200m in public funds being spent to upgrade security at Nkandla, including the need to protect the residence from earthquakes, floods, disease and violent attacks.

The passing of Nelson Mandela on 5 December 2013 sent the nation and, it sometimes seemed, the entire world into an intense period of mourning.

Zapiro refreshed a cartoon that first appeared on Mandela's departure from politics in 1999.

President Barack Obama's soaring oratory at the Mandela commemoration at Soccer City contrasted starkly with the ponderous script poorly delivered by Zuma after he had been booed by some parts of the crowd.

The unqualified Thamsanqa Jantjie had somehow been employed to interpret for the deaf at the Mandela commemoration and found himself at the centre of global condemnation for his incomprehensible hand gestures.

In January 2014, Helen Zille thought she had a "game-changer" three months ahead of the election when she announced that Agang's Mamphela Ramphele would run as the DA's presidential candidate but the deal unravelled within 48 hours of political chaos, back-tracking and recrimination.

Julius Malema was turning up the heat on Gwede Mantashe's ANC.

At a joint media conference, IFP leader Mangosuthu Buthelezi "wholeheartedly accepted" an apology from Malema for once calling him a "factory fault" and describing his party as "a terrorist organisation".

Helen Zille's very active presence on Twitter provoked more trouble for the DA leader when she launched a vitriolic attack on *City Press* journalist Carien du Plessis claiming she was "so terrified that she will be damned by her own complexion that she has to bend over to prove her political correctness".

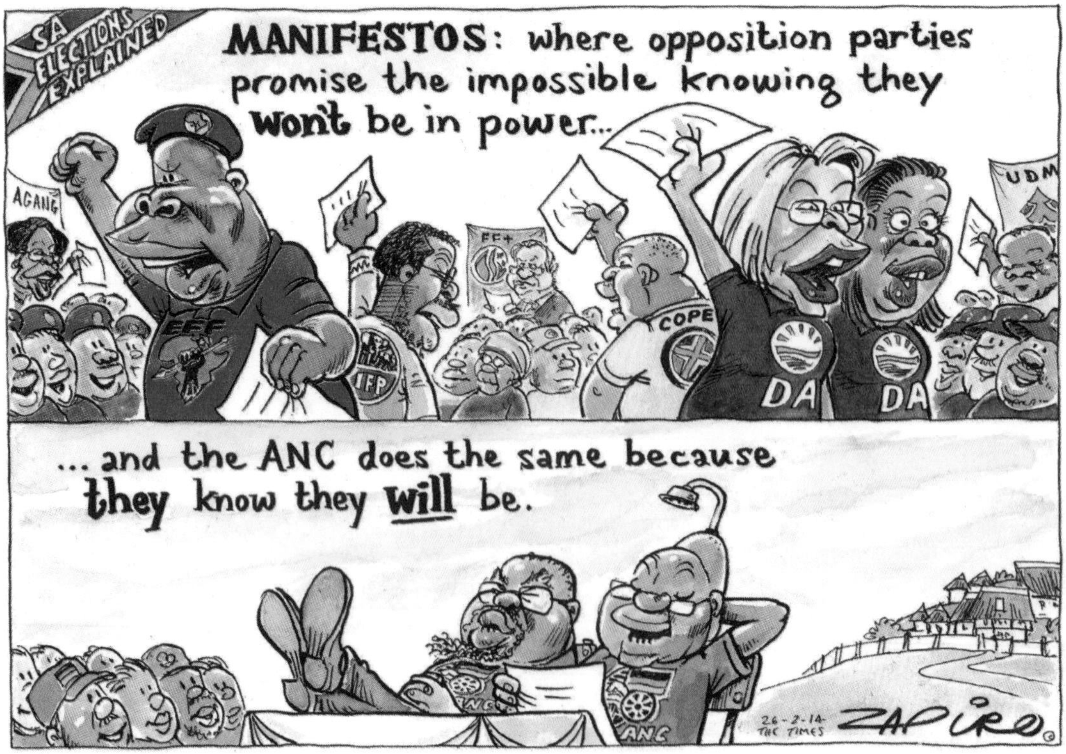
SA ELECTIONS EXPLAINED
MANIFESTOS: where opposition parties promise the impossible knowing they won't be in power...
AGANG
EFF
IFP
FF+
COPE
DA
DA
UDM
... and the ANC does the same because they know they will be.
ANC
ANC
26-2-14 THE TIMES
ZAPIRO

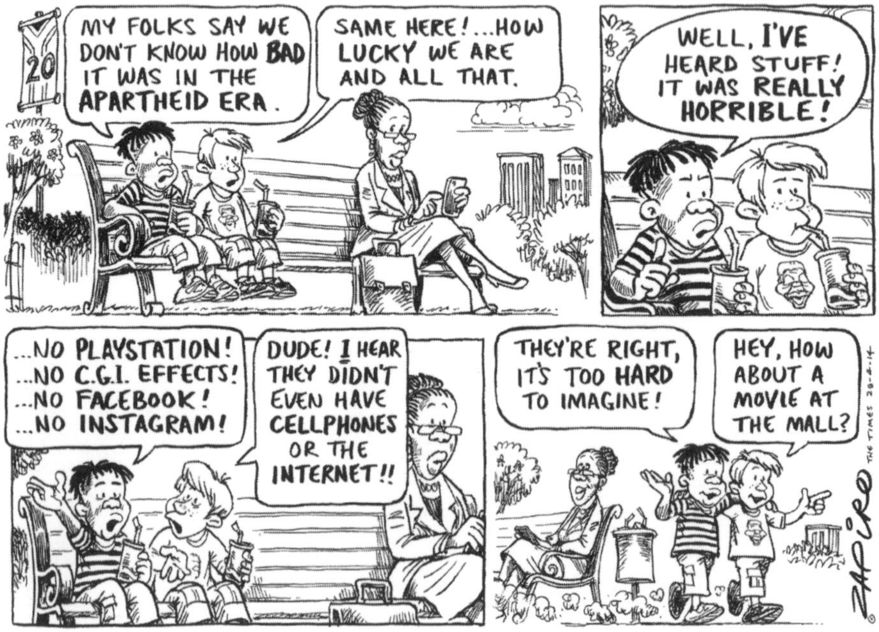
20
MY FOLKS SAY WE DON'T KNOW HOW BAD IT WAS IN THE APARTHEID ERA.
SAME HERE!...HOW LUCKY WE ARE AND ALL THAT.
WELL, I'VE HEARD STUFF! IT WAS REALLY HORRIBLE!
...NO PLAYSTATION! ...NO C.G.I. EFFECTS! ...NO FACEBOOK! ...NO INSTAGRAM!
DUDE! I HEAR THEY DIDN'T EVEN HAVE CELLPHONES OR THE INTERNET!!
THEY'RE RIGHT, IT'S TOO HARD TO IMAGINE!
HEY, HOW ABOUT A MOVIE AT THE MALL?
THE TIMES 28-4-14
ZAPIRO

Three prominent members of the old ANC guard, Kgalema Motlanthe, Trevor Manuel and Ben Turok, were leaving parliament, and Rivonia Triallist Andrew Mlangeni spoke out against corruption and entitlement.

Former intelligence minister Ronnie Kasrils and over 100 other disillusioned ANC supporters launched the 'Sidikiwe! Vukani! Vote No!' campaign because of personal greed and self-enrichment in government.

Just weeks before the election, Public Protector Thuli Madonsela released her damning report on the "unconscionable" Nkandla spending which included the infamous 'fire pool', a cattle kraal and a chicken run. She found that Jacob Zuma and his family had benefitted personally from the spending.

Madonsela's report caused a flutter in the security cluster of ministers who had been defending the president on the issue.

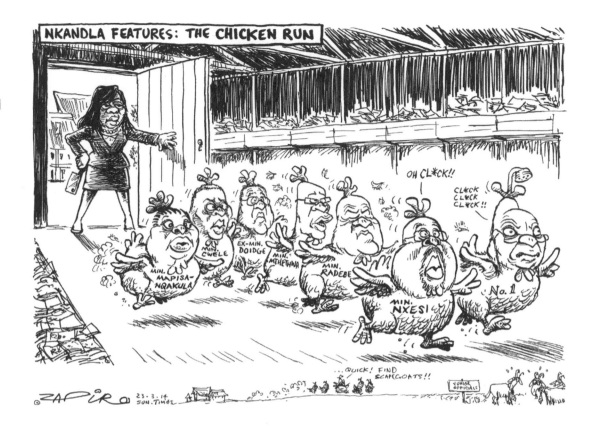

The DA sent out a text stating that Madonsela's report showed "how Zuma stole your money". The Johannesburg High Court rejected an ANC claim that this was false information in contravention of the Electoral Act, ruling that a phrase in the report, "licence to loot", meant the SMS constituted fair comment. The Electoral Court would later rule differently.

DAY 11: WILL POLICE BUNGLING PREVENT JUSTICE FOR REEVA?!!

MARIKANA INQUIRY, MONTH 19:
...MORE EVIDENCE THAT POLICE PLANTED WEAPONS...
...SWEPT CRIME SCENE TO REMOVE THEIR OWN WEAPONS...
...DOCTORED INCRIMINATING VIDEOS...
...MURDERED MINERS IN COLD BLOOD AS THEY SURRENDERED...
...LEFT THE WOUNDED TO DIE...
...THE INVESTIGATION WAS CONDUCTED BY THE VERY COPS WHO DID THE KILLING....

THE TIMES 17·3·14 ZAPIRO

The Oscar Pistorius murder trial finally got underway in Pretoria in March 2014 under the glare of an intense media spotlight which was conspicuously absent from more important matters.

As Pistorius was on the witness stand, Shrien Dewani was, after lengthy procedural delays, extradited from the UK to Cape Town to stand trial for organising the murder of his new wife, Anni, in Gugulethu in November 2010.

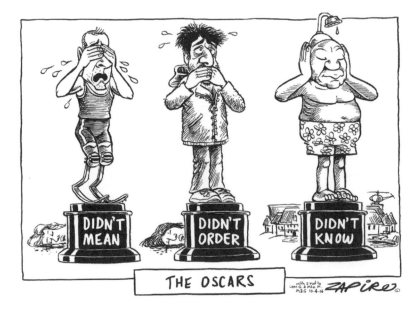

Freedom Day, 2014.

Archbishop Emeritus Desmond Tutu expressed disappointment with the ANC, saying he didn't support the party the way he did 20 years ago.

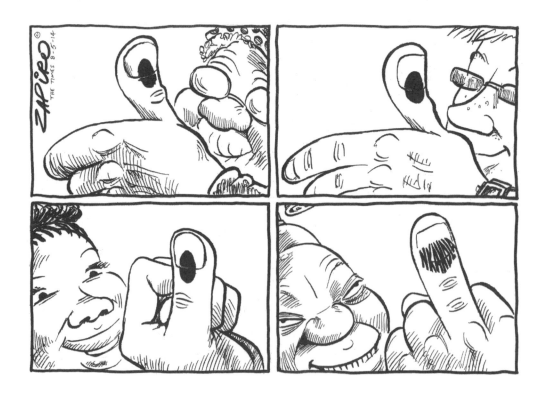

On election day 2014 the aggressive new kid on the block, Julius Malema's EFF, garnered significant backing at the polls.

The ANC defied the sceptics and attracted 62% of the vote but some cracks definitely had appeared in support for the party of liberation.

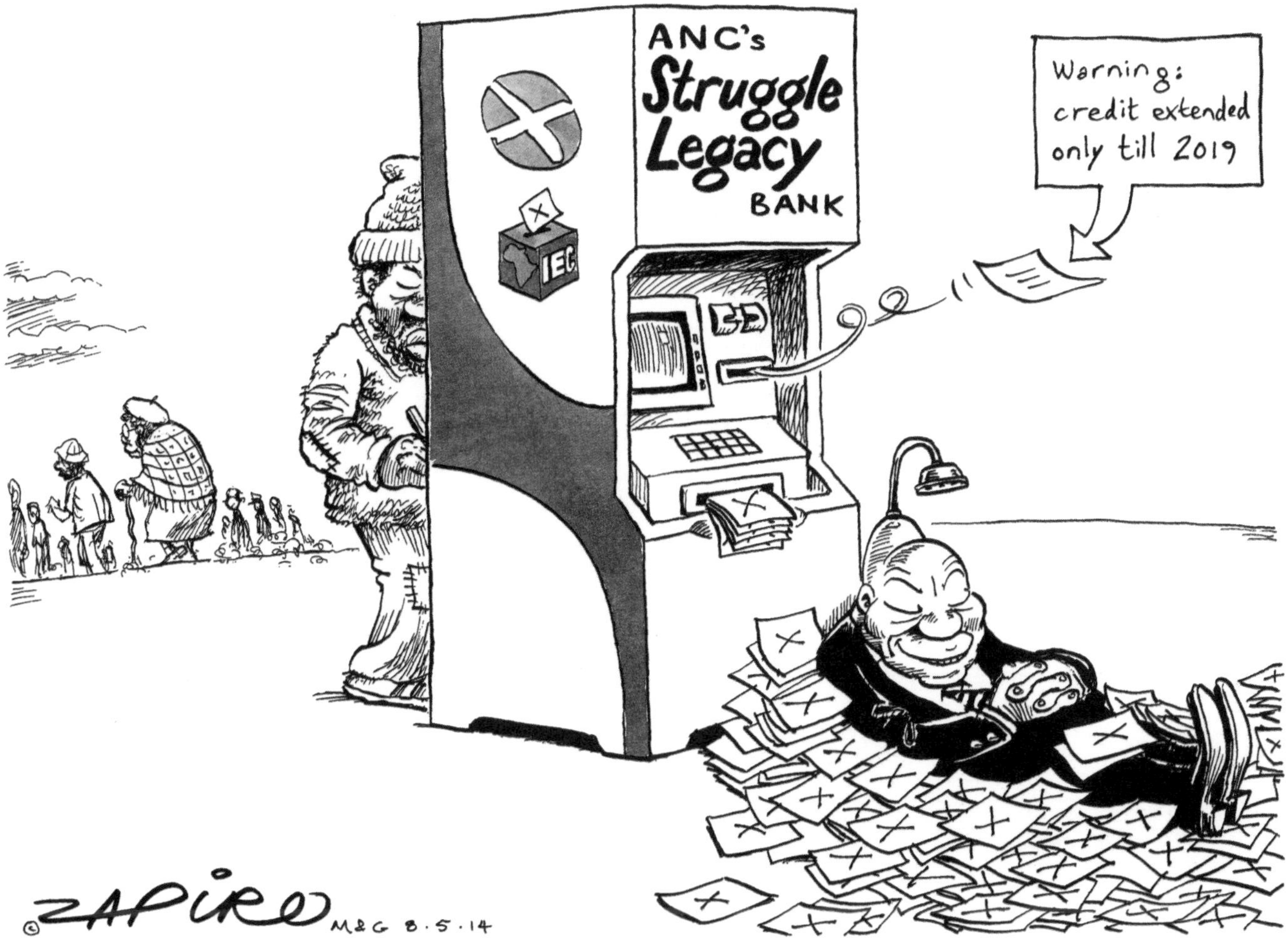
ANC's
Struggle
Legacy
BANK
Warning:
credit extended
only till 2019
IEC
©ZAPIRO M&G 8.5.14

CARTOON ANNUALS BY ZAPIRO

The Madiba Years (1996)
The Hole Truth (1997)
End of Part One (1998)
Call Mr Delivery (1999)
The Devil Made Me Do It! (2000)
The ANC Went in 4X4 (2001)
Bushwhacked (2002)
Dr Do-Little and the African Potato (2003)
Long Walk to Free Time (2004)
Is There a Spin Doctor In the House? (2005)
Da Zuma Code (2006)
Take Two Veg and Call Me in the Morning (2007)
Pirates of Polokwane (2008)
Don't Mess With the President's Head (2009)
Do You Know Who I Am?! (2010)
The Last Sushi (2011)
But Will It Stand Up in Court? (2012)
My Big Fat Gupta Wedding (2013)

OTHER PUBLICATIONS

The Mandela Files (2008)
VuvuzelaNation (2013)

10 Orange Street
Sunnyside
Auckland Park 2092
South Africa
+27 11 628 3200

In association with

© Jonathan Shapiro, 2014
Text © Mike Wills, 2014

ISBN 978-1-4314-1036-1

Cover design by Zapiro
Page layout by MR Design

Colouring done by Zapiro with the exception of:
Roberto – the cover, pages 42, 69, 70, 81, 82,
105, 113, 117, 139, 140, 148, 171, 172, 174,
175, 176, 192, 197, 224, 236, 241;
Andrew Putter – pages 8, 16, 17, 18, 19, 22, 26,
27, 52, 53, 56, 71, 90, 92.

First, second and third impression 2014

Printed by Creda Communications
Job no. 002298

See a complete list of Jacana titles at
www.jacana.co.za